BRE

LEARN to
DRIVE

IN *10* easy STAGES

THIRD EDITION

LEARN to DRIVE

IN *10* easy STAGES

PASS RATES OF OVER DOUBLE THE NATIONAL AVERAGE ACHIEVED IN FIELD TRIALS

Margaret Stacey

ILLUSTRATED BY ANDY RICE

First published in 1987
Reprinted 1987, 1988 (twice), 1989
Revised edition 1990
Reprinted 1991
Second edition published in 1993
Reprinted with revisions 1994
Reprinted 1995, 1996
Revised edition 1998
Third edition published in 1999
Reprinted 2001
Reprinted 2002

ISBN 0 7494 3019 2

Kogan Page Limited, 120 Pentonville Road, London N1 9JN

British Library Cataloguing in Publication Data

A CIP record for this book is available from the British Library.

Typeset by Oliver Hickey
Printed and bound by Thanet Press Ltd, Margate, Kent

Contents

About the author

Margaret Stacey runs a successful driving instructor training establishment in Derbyshire. She is the co-author of the bestselling **Driving Instructor's Handbook**, which is recommended to instructors by the Department of Transport; **Practical Teaching Skills for Driving Instructors**, now being used by new and experienced instructors for improving their teaching skills, and **The Advanced Driver's Handbook**, incorporated by many instructors throughout the UK and Ireland as part of their defensive driving courses. She has also co-authored **How to Pass the New Theory L Test**, which covers the entire syllabus of the theory test. All of these titles are published by Kogan Page. Margaret also publishes a Home Study Programme for those studying for the Approved Driving Instructor examination and this is also used on licence by many other training establishments. She is currently serving on several national committees relating to the driving instruction industry.

Acknowledgements

My thanks go to all of those ADIs who use this book; particularly those who have taken the time to pass on to me their thanks and constructive comments.

Introduction

This book has been written by ADIs (Approved Driving Instructors) recognized as leading trainers within the industry.

It is a comprehensive course designed to help provisional licence holders prepare for both the theory and practical parts of the driving test and is linked to the DSA (Driving Standards Agency) recommended syllabus for learner drivers.

One of the most common reasons for test failure is insufficient preparation and practice. The DSA recommends that the best way of learning to drive is to have lessons with an ADI and supplement this with plenty of practice.

This book has been written to:

- help you with your studies for the theory test;

- supplement your practical driving lessons;

- provide guidance for you and your supervisor when you are practising.

It shows you:

- what to expect on your lessons;

- how to develop driving as a life skill;

- what you need to know to pass the theory test, and practical driving test.

Reducing the risk of accidents

A high percentage of newly-qualified drivers are involved in accidents. Under the New Driver Act, if you accumulate more than six penalty points within two years of passing your test, you will have to:

- go back to using a provisional licence;

- display 'L' plates; and

- take another driving test.

This book explains how to develop your control skills so that you will be able to handle your car safely and efficiently. This will make learning to drive an enjoyable experience.

Your instructor will explain how to apply the rules you are learning and teach you to plan ahead and anticipate what could happen. This will help you to learn how to avoid problems of conflict with other road users, which in turn will help you keep your full licence and enjoy 'safe driving for life'.

How to use this programme

Organizing your course of training

This training programme has now been in use for many years. Those following it consistently achieve driving test pass rates of well over double the national average.

By following this programme, and combining learning the theory with your practical lessons, you will soon learn how to apply the rules to different road situations more easily.

Learn to Drive in 10 Easy Stages includes common-sense advice starting with how to choose your instructor and progressing to changing a wheel. These stages will enable you to plan and pace yourself according to your own natural aptitude and driving ability.

Charting your progress

The systematic step-by-step programme of learning in this book is designed to take the panic and confusion out of your practice and therefore make more effective use of your time.

You can map your progress through the course by ticking the appropriate boxes at the end of each stage of learning.

Key points

Each stage identifies key learning points. Before your lesson, study these points carefully along with any relevant Highway Code rules. If your next session is private practice get your supervisor to study the key points and the rules as well. Read the introduction to each stage and follow the instructions carefully.

The DSA syllabus for learners

The book **The Driving Test** has been compiled by the Driving Standards Agency. Their motto is 'Safe Driving for Life'. The book contains their recommended syllabus for learning to drive. Read the pages listed at the beginning of each stage of **Learn to Drive** and make sure you get lots of practice at all of the skills involved.

Complete the checkpoint
Before each practical lesson, complete the checkpoint. Tick the most appropriate answers in pencil or on a separate piece of paper. Match them with the answers at the end of the book and record your scores.

Using illustrations to help you understand
Most of the key learning points are illustrated with diagrams. This will help you to:

- understand more easily;

- recognize risks earlier;

- predict danger; and

- avoid conflict with other road users.

Learning in stages
Try to follow the sequence of the stages, making sure you have learned and practised all of the points before going on to the next.

Sometimes the area you live in may mean that some topics will need to be covered in a different sequence. For example, if you live near roundabouts and dual carriage-ways you will have to be taught how to drive on them fairly early on in your course of lessons.

The manoeuvre exercises can be introduced at any point. However, it is advisable that your clutch control skills are fairly well developed before you start learning how to reverse as you will be more confident and achieve success more easily.

Using this guide as your personal logbook

When learning something new, your instructor/supervisor should begin by giving you a full explanation and 'talk-through' practice. As your skill improves, you should progress and carry out the various tasks with less assistance. Finally, you should be able to complete the exercises without any help at all.

There are tick boxes at the end of each learning programme to help you chart your progress. You can get your instructor and supervisor to help by adding their constructive comments in the spaces provided.

Keep practising each skill until you and your instructor are happy with your progress and then proceed on to the next topic.

In car lessons and practice

You must feel confident in yourself. Be prepared to take your instructor's advice and have enough lessons and practice on all of the subjects covered.

If you are unsure of anything or don't understand the reasons for it, ask your instructor to go over it again. Remember you must feel confident that you can carry out the skills reasonably well if you want to become safe and efficient and also enjoy your driving.

Concentration

It is important that you maintain your concentration all of the time. When learning a new skill the initial practising time should be limited to about 15 minutes. Take a short break to discuss your performance and then practise again. Following this system will help you keep your concentration and therefore make your learning more effective.

Recap at the start of each lesson

At the beginning of each lesson or practice session, your instructor or supervisor should spend a few minutes going over what you learnt previously. Not only will this confirm whether or not you know and understand the rules and procedures, but it will also help in your preparation for the theory test.

Keeping a check on appointments and progress

Your instructor may use a special appointment/progress card like the one illustrated in the back of this book. This will not only be a reminder of your lesson appointments but it will also give you feedback of your progress and highlight where you need more practice.

You can keep your own record of your progress by filling in the 'Can Do' statements on page 225.

The driving test

There are two parts to the driving test: the theory test, and the practical test.

The theory test

You can apply for this as soon as you have received and signed your provisional driving licence. Your instructor should be able to supply you with an application form, or you can get one from the local driving test centre. Theory test centres are listed on the form.

You can take the theory test before you begin your driving lessons. However, it is sensible to study for the theory test and have your driving lessons at the same time. Your instructor will then be able to teach you how to apply the rules and procedures in real situations. This will make it easier for you to understand them.

The test consists of 35 multiple choice questions covering all of the subjects dealt with in this book.

Full details of what you will need to take with you when you attend for the test will be included with your test appointment confirmation letter.

When you pass, you will be issued with a certificate. You must enter the certificate number on your practical test application form. You must also remember to take the certificate with you when you attend for your driving test.

A theory test pass certificate is valid for two years. You must pass the driving test within the two-year period, otherwise you will have to take the theory part again.

The practical test

When you have passed the theory test, take your instructor's advice and only apply for the practical when you are told you will be ready. It could also shorten the length of time between the theory and practical tests, if you start having your driving lessons while studying for the theory test.

Be prepared to have enough professional driving tuition. It is far better to be properly prepared and pass first time than be disappointed!

Remember, a failed test means extra cost in terms of:

- another test fee;

- more driving lessons;

- time – there may be a long waiting list for tests at your local centre.

The test content is given in detail in the DSA book **The Driving Test**. Your instructor should cover the recommended syllabus for learning which it contains.

The 'Pass Plus' scheme

When you have passed both parts of the driving test, it means that you have achieved the minimum standard required to drive on the road unaccompanied.

It is sensible to get extra tuition in topics you may not have covered while preparing for your driving test. Many driving instructors now offer this service under the Pass Plus scheme.

You should at least be prepared to have some lessons on motorway driving while under the safe supervision of a professional.

Topics included in the Pass Plus scheme are listed in Stage 10 of this book.

Before you drive

Introduction

This section gives you advice on how to choose a driving instructor and about practice with friends and relatives. It also tells you things you need to know before you drive on the road.

The most effective way of preparing for both parts of your driving test is to combine the theory with the practice. To help you learn 'safe driving for life' and to prepare you for the theory test, you need to be studying the following books: **The Highway Code; The Driving Test; The Driving Manual and How to Prepare for the Theory 'L' Test.**

These books will help you to understand the rules so that you can apply them during your practical lessons. If your driving instructor does not have all of them in stock, you should be able to buy them at any good book shop.

Before driving you should read **The Driving Manual** – Part 1: The Driver; and Part 2: The Driver and the Law; **The Driving Test** – Part 1, pages 4–11 and Part 6, pages 79–85.

These sections explain all about the driving test, how to apply for each part and the recommended syllabus for learning to drive.

The Highway Code

Understanding what the rules mean will help you put them into practice safely. Your instructor should help you learn how to apply the rules in different situations.

Before you drive you need to study the following rules:

43	Animals in your car
72	Vehicle condition
75–77	Seat belts
78	Children in cars

When you have studied the rules, work through this stage and complete the checkpoint at the end of it. Your instructor should help if you have any problems or don't understand some of the rules.

Choosing a driving instructor

The only official qualification for driving instructors is: Driving Standards Agency Approved Driving Instructor (Car).

Your instructor should display a certificate in the left-hand side of the windscreen. It shows:

- the official green ADI badge;

- the instructor's photograph;

- his or her ADI number;

- date of issue and date of expiry.

An instructor's certificate

If there is a red triangular badge on display, this means that the instructor is a 'Licensed Trainee Driving Instructor' who is waiting to take the final part of the qualifying examination.

Ask around and go to an instructor who has a good reputation and a high pass rate. Have a chat with the instructor before committing yourself. This will help establish whether you will feel at ease and can communicate easily.

Ask for an outline of the course and check that it covers the syllabus in The Driving Test. If you are in doubt, think carefully about paying out large sums in advance.

Safe driving for life

Remember that you are investing in something that is going to help keep you safe on the road for the rest of your life. You will have to be able to cope on your own in today's very busy and sometimes complicated road systems. The 'L' test is only a very basic minimum standard.

> Do not fall into the trap of wanting to have as few lessons as possible and at the cheapest possible price!

Learning to drive today is much more complicated than it was 20 years ago. Don't be influenced by older drivers saying: 'I only had six lessons!' The number of lessons you will need depends not only on your instructor's skills, but also on your age, your ability to learn and how much regular practice you are able to get.

To calculate how many lessons you are likely to need, you should multiply your age by two. However, this is only an average — you may learn more quickly or you may need more lessons — everyone is different!

After passing your test your instructor may offer you extra training under the Pass Plus scheme. Take advantage of this as you will be able to gain experience in a wider variety of situations, for example driving at night and on motorways.

Do I need to learn quickly?

One of the most effective ways of learning is to have two or three lessons each week with practice in between. As you have to pass the theory test before you can apply for the practical driving test, combining your lessons with your studies helps you prepare for both elements at the same time.

However, some people need to learn more quickly, for example if a job depends on having a driving licence. You will still have to pass the theory test first.

If you are considering an intensive course you need to bear in mind that driving test appointments have to be booked in advance. It is sensible to arrange for an assessment before you make your decision. This will help your instructor to establish whether or not you have the ability to learn quickly and will be up to the required standard in time.

The cost of learning

The quality of tuition varies as much as price! Choosing the wrong instructor, because lessons are cheap, may cost you more in the long run.

Go for quality, not quantity.

Go for quality, not quantity

Work out for yourself the cost of 30 lessons at £17.00 against that of 70 at £7.50. Not only is it costing more but it is also taking twice as long to learn!

Are you learning already?

If you are already learning to drive but are not quite sure about the quality of training you are getting, ask yourself the following questions.

Does my instructor:

- give an outline of the course?

- arrive on time for my lessons?

- behave professionally?

- help me with my studies for the theory test?

- recap on my previous lesson?

- explain what we're going to do at the start of lessons?

- explain things in simple and understandable terms?

- demonstrate when I don't understand?

- assess my progress and give me feedback?

- praise me when I get things right?

- help me to understand when I get things wrong?

- fill in my progress card or logbook for each lesson?

- allow me to ask questions without feeling awkward?

- tell me what to study before the next lesson?

- show a real interest in my progress?

If you have a good instructor, you should have been able to answer yes to most of these questions. If you can't, then you should try to discuss the problems. If you are offered no remedy, you should perhaps consider looking for another driving instructor. Remember – it's your money and your choice.

If you feel you have a justifiable complaint, write to The Registrar – ADI, The Driving Standards Agency, Stanley House, 56 Talbot Street, Nottingham NG1 5GU.

Practising with friends and relatives

The DSA recommend that you get plenty of practice to supplement your lessons. However, before you do this you should have some lessons with your instructor. Listen to the advice given and only start practising when your instructor tells you that you are confident enough and can control the car without problems.

If you are practising with anyone who is not a qualified driving instructor, by law your supervisor must be over 21 and have held a full UK driving licence for at least three years for the group of vehicle you will be driving.

Not all drivers make good instructors. If you are taught bad habits at the start, they may stay with you for a long time. You might also become confused if your supervisor is telling you different things from your instructor. This confusion can often lead to needing more lessons in the long run. By studying this book with you, your supervisor should be able to guide your practice so that it speeds up your progress using up-to-date methods and following the latest rules.

Responding angrily can lead to further argument

Very often, close relatives and friends are too personally involved and may become over-anxious and agitated. If you feel you are being told off unjustly – try to stay calm. Responding angrily will only lead to further argument and loss of concentration. This will not help your progress.

Making it legal to drive

When your instructor says you are ready for extra practice, make sure that you, your supervisor and the car you will be driving, are properly insured.

The minimum age for driving a small passenger vehicle is normally 17. It is 16 if you are in receipt of a mobility

Ensure that you are properly insured

allowance. You can apply for your provisional licence up to two months before you want it to start. You must not drive until you have received and signed it. A provisional licence allows you to drive only under the supervision of an ADI or a qualified driver.

Remember it is illegal to give payment of any kind, either in money or goods, to anyone supervising your driving unless they are on the Register of Approved Driving Instructors.

Make sure the vehicle you are driving is taxed. The disc should be displayed in the front nearside of the windscreen.

Alcohol and drugs

If you are taking medicines or drugs, ask your doctor if they are likely to affect your driving. Even some common cough remedies can cause drowsiness — read the directions carefully. If in doubt, ask the chemist.

Drinking and taking certain drugs can affect your driving

Alcohol is a drug. It can make you feel over-confident and less aware of danger. It makes people think they can achieve the impossible and blurs judgement of speed and distance. Even small amounts of alcohol will slow down your reactions.

If you drink the night before a lesson, the amount of alcohol in your body may still exceed the legal limit in the morning!

Keeping your practice safe

The car in which you practise is unlikely to have dual controls – don't be tempted to try too much too soon. Avoid problems by asking your supervisor to select routes that you will be able to cope with. Your supervisor should also help by planning well ahead.

Ask for instructions and directions to be given in plenty of time so that you can carry them out without rushing. If things get too complicated your supervisor should be prepared to compensate, for example with steering corrections or by applying the handbrake.

Being a learner is no excuse for breaking the law — careless driving could result in disqualification for you and your supervisor. Make sure that you are able to stop under control before you drive in traffic. If you feel you can't cope ask your supervisor to take over.

Your instructor should advise you on the parts of this book to study with your supervisor before going out to practise. Make sure that you both understand what you are going to do. It may also help if your supervisor sits in the back of the school car to see what stage you have reached.

If you find something is too difficult, ask for a further explanation or a demonstration. If you still have difficulty in understanding or carrying out a routine, ask your instructor to work on it with you on your next lesson.

Avoid unnecessary journeys in bad weather

During the early stages of learning, avoid driving in bad weather conditions. You already have enough to concentrate on! Your early lessons and practice should be in areas where you can concentrate on learning to control the car. When you can control the car properly, you should get as much practice on as many different types of road and in as many different conditions as possible.

Is your vehicle roadworthy?

If the vehicle you are driving is over three years old, it must undergo an annual MOT test. Check the test certificate. Although the car has passed the MOT on the day of the test, it does not mean that the car is still roadworthy!

Before getting in, check the tyres to see whether they are properly inflated. Check for stones in the tread, and look for any cuts or bulges in the rubber. You should also make sure that the following are working: indicators, all of the lights, and the horn.

Scratched or dirty windows make driving difficult. Glare from bright sunlight and the headlights of other vehicles can make vision distorted and painful to the eyes. Use water and a soft cloth or leather to clean the windows inside and out. Make sure the lights and mirrors are clean.

Use a leather or soft cloth to clean the windows

Condensation can restrict your vision, particularly in damp or cold weather. Do not drive away if any of the windows are steamed up. Clear the windows before driving with a leather or with the demister and rear screen heater. A slightly open window can help prevent condensation from re-forming once you are on the move.

Reducing distractions when driving

To maintain your concentration you must be comfortable when driving. Visit the toilet before your lessons. Get ready in plenty of time so that you can spend a few minutes relaxing. This will help you collect your thoughts and prepare yourself mentally for driving.

Try to avoid any arguments before going out — they will put you in the wrong mood for driving and learning.

Avoid arguments before a driving lesson

When practising, it is not a good idea to put 'L' plates in the windows — they could create blind spots and restrict your view of the road. Remove any unnecessary stickers and toy mascots, which may also cause blind spots and distractions.

It is not normally a good idea to carry extra passengers during the early stages of learning. It could affect your concentration. If this is unavoidable, make sure they get in safely and sit where they will not restrict your view in the mirrors.

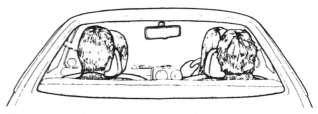

Make sure that passengers do not obstruct your view

Children can get bored travelling in cars. This will make it difficult for you to concentrate on your driving. If they must go with you, make sure they are properly restrained and kept under control. This also applies if you take your pets in the car.

Children should be restrained and under control

Before driving away, check for any loose articles that might distract you. Tidy up maps, papers or other items lying around. If they move about while you are driving, they could distract you and cause you to have an accident.

Loose articles could contribute to an accident

Make sure there is nothing on the floor likely to roll around, such as a child's toy or an aerosol can. Apart from being a distraction, they could roll under the pedals and prevent you from applying the brakes properly.

Debris on the floor could restrict pedal use

Getting ready for your first driving lesson

The concentration needed when driving can be quite tiring, especially in the early stages of learning. You will need plenty of fresh air to help you stay alert. During cold weather you should keep the temperature comfortable – but not too warm. A slightly open window can help.

Wear light, comfortable clothes. Most car heating systems are very effective – heavy coats are unnecessary and could restrict your arm movements making it difficult to turn the steering wheel. Avoid tight fitting clothes that may be uncomfortable when driving as this could either distract you or restrict body movement.

Wear comfortable clothing

Fashion shoes are not suitable for driving

Flat shoes are normally the best for driving. Heavy boots or fashion shoes may make controlling the pedals difficult. The ridged soles of some trainers can catch on the pedals and make your driving jerky.

Check your eyesight

When you apply for your provisional driving licence, you sign to the effect that you can read a number plate from a distance of 20.5 metres (67 feet). Make sure that you can.

In today's busy conditions you need to be looking well ahead. If you need your glasses to read the number plate, you must also wear them for driving. If you are in doubt get your eyes tested professionally.

You need to be able to read a number plate from 20.5 metres

Checkpoint

Before going out to practise, answer the following questions. Some of them will have more than one correct answer. If you can't answer some of them, or you don't understand what they mean, refer back to the books or Highway Code rules listed at the beginning of this Stage. If you still don't understand — ask your instructor.

1   An ADI's certificate is:
   a. blue
   b. green
   c. red
   d. yellow

2   Anyone supervising a learner driver must be:
   a. 18 and have passed the L test
   b. 18 and have held a full licence for six months
   c. 21 and have held a full licence for six months
   d. 21 and have held a full licence for three years

3   Before applying for your theory test you must:
   a. apply for your driving licence
   b. apply for your practical driving test
   c. have at least 10 driving lessons
   d. have received and signed your licence ✓

4 Anyone supervising a learner driver must have held a full licence for:
a. six months
b. one year
c. two years
d. three years

5 When you pass your theory test, you will be given:
a. an award
b. a practical test application form
c. a pass certificate
d. a diploma

6 If you receive a mobility allowance, the minimum age at which you can drive is:
a. 15
b. 16
c. 17
d. 18

7 Unless you receive a mobility allowance, the minimum age for driving is:
a. 15
b. 16
c. 17-
d. 18

8 To meet the legal eyesight requirements, you should be able to read a number plate from:
a. 10.5 metres
b. 15.5 metres
c. 17.5 metres
d. 20.5 metres

9 To be sure your driving won't be affected if you are taking prescribed medicine, ask your:
a. ADI
b. supervisor
c. community worker
d. doctor

10 Cars used for driving lessons should be:
a. fitted with dual controls
b. roadworthy
c. less than three years old
d. saloon models

11 'L' plates must be displayed on the car:
    a. on the bonnet and boot
    b. clearly to the front and rear
    c. in the front and rear windows
    d. on a properly constructed roof sign

12 Cars being driven on the road must display a:
    a. valid tax disc
    b. valid MOT certificate
    c. roadworthiness certificate
    d. insurance certificate

13 If you have been drinking the night before a driving lesson, in the morning you:
    a. should be all right to drive
    b. could still be over the limit
    c. should have more confidence
    d. should ask your ADI to test your breath

14 Loose articles in the car could:
    a. distract the driver
    b. prevent a pedal from being used properly
    c. be convenient for use in an emergency
    d. help entertain any child passengers

15 A theory test pass certificate is valid for:
    a. six months
    b. one year
    c. 18 months
    d. two years

16 You can apply for your practical test when you have:
    a. applied for the theory test
    b. had a minimum of 10 lessons
    c. passed the theory test
    d. read the Highway Code and Driving Manual

17 People exempted from wearing seat belts are:
    a. holders of medical exemption certificates
    b. long distance lorry drivers
    c. driving instructors
    d. driving examiners
    e. those making local deliveries in special vehicles

18 The driver is responsible for the wearing of seat belts by:
   a. all passengers, regardless of age
   b. children over 14 but under 16
   c. all children under 14
   d. any adult with a disability

19 You must report to the DVLA any:
   a. diabetes controlled by insulin or tablets
   b. serious problem with memory
   c. any diabetic condition
   d. fractured limbs

20 The most effective ways to counter sleepiness when driving are:
   a. avoid driving in the dark
   b. avoid driving for more than two hours at a time
   c. keeping fresh air circulating in the car
   d. taking regular breaks

21 You must not drive with a blood alcohol level higher than:
   a. 60mg/80ml
   b. 75mg/90ml
   c. 80mg/100ml
   d. 80mg/120ml

22 Driving after drinking alcohol will:
   a. give you a false sense of confidence
   b. speed up your reaction time
   c. make you more likely to take risks
   d. slow down your reactions
   e. affect your judgement

23 At night, you must use:
   a. sidelights only, in built up areas
   b. headlights, except on restricted roads
   c. headlights when visibility is reduced
   d. fog lights at all times to help others see you

24 When dazzled by oncoming headlights, you should:
   a. flash the other driver
   b. slow down or stop
   c. brake quickly until you can see properly again
   d. sound your horn as a warning

25 Hazard warning lights may be used when you are:
   a. stationary and causing an obstruction
   b. on a motorway and there is a hazard ahead
   c. parking for under 15 minutes on yellow lines
   d. being towed or are towing another vehicle

26 Before overtaking another car, you should:
   a. switch on your full beam to warn others
   b. keep your headlights dipped
   c. switch on the hazard flashers
   d. keep flashing the headlights

27 Be prepared to adapt your driving. You should:
   a. always treat speed limits as targets
   b. be prepared for vehicles emerging from junctions
   c. use the horn whenever you see pedestrians
   d. be prepared for pedestrians to step into the road at any time

28 An MOT certificate is needed for cars which have been registered for:
   a. 18 months
   b. two years
   c. two and a half years
   d. three years

29 Before driving you must:
   a. have received and signed your driving licence
   b. have applied for your driving licence
   c. have passed your theory test
   d. have a medical and eyesight test

30 A full driving licence is valid until your:
   a. 60th birthday
   b. 65th birthday
   c. 70th birthday
   d. retirement

You will find the answers on page 221

Scores: 1st try [   ]; 2nd try [   ]; 3rd try [   ].

Record your scores in the appendix on page 225.

Get to know your car

Read **The Driving Manual** – Part 3: The Controls; Part 4: Driving Mirrors.
Read pages 21–26 of **The Driving Test**.
Revise **Highway Code** rules 75 and 76 – seat belts.

This lesson will give you the chance to get the feel of the main controls and to practise some simple exercises before you get the car moving. Make sure you understand and can carry out the following instructions in a stationary car before going on to Stage 3.

The instruction	What it means
Cover the clutch	Place your left foot over the pedal without touching it.
Cover the brake	Place your right foot over the pedal without touching it.
Set the gas	Press the gas (accelerator) gently to increase the engine speed to a steady 'tickover' speed.
Find the 'holding point'	Let the clutch pedal up slowly until you hear the engine slow down a little and then keep your foot still. This is often called the 'biting point'.

After learning the above instructions, work through the rest of the stage and complete the checkpoint before going out to practise.

As you work your way through, you will find other instructions you will need to understand before moving off, for example: 'Select 1st gear' and 'Take the handbrake off'.

Getting into the 'cockpit drill' habit

1. Doors

Opening a door carelessly can put you or others in danger. It may force them to brake or swerve, causing an accident.

Get into your car as quickly as possible, close the door and listen to make sure that any passengers have closed theirs properly. Check in the nearside and offside mirrors that the doors are flush with the bodyline of the car. Remember – you are responsible for the safety of your passengers. A door not closed properly will rattle. It could fly open as you drive along or go around a bend. Also check that the handbrake is firmly on.

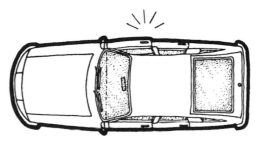

An open door can be dangerous

2. Seat

If your seat is not properly adjusted you will not be able to reach the controls and use them properly. If you are uncomfortable you will not be able to concentrate properly. Both of these situations could result in danger.

To position yourself for driving comfortably you need to sit up with your bottom well back in the seat. Make sure you can see clearly ahead, if you need more height use a properly secured cushion.

Using your left foot push the clutch pedal (the one on the left) fully down to the floor. You should have just a slight bend in the knee. If you get too close you may find it awkward to raise the clutch or to control it properly.

To reach the wheel properly, position your hands at between 'ten to two' and 'a quarter to three'. Keeping each hand on its own half of the wheel, you should be able to slide your hands easily from the top to the bottom and back again. There should be just a slight bend in your elbows and you should be able to use the wheel while keeping your elbows clear of your body.

Position your hands between 10 to 2 or quarter to 3

If you find this awkward, you could be sitting with the top half of your body too close to the wheel and may need to adjust the back rake of the seat. If you do this, make sure that you can still reach the clutch pedal.

When you have adjusted the seat and can reach all of the main controls comfortably, you should position the head restraint so that it will protect your head and neck.

3. Mirrors

The driving mirrors are extremely important aids. No action should be taken without having first assessed what effect it will have on other road users. Your instructor will teach you how to get into the mirror–signal–manoeuvre habit.

Adjust the interior mirror so that you can see clearly to the rear without having to move your head. Hold it as shown in the diagram, keeping your fingers off the glass. Line up the top edge with the top of the rear window and the offside (driver's) side down the right side of the rear window.

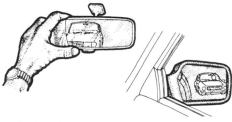

Adjusting the interior mirror

The door mirrors help to reduce the blind areas to the sides of the car. You will need to use these before changing direction, for example, before moving off, turning left and right, passing parked vehicles, when changing lanes, etc.

Adjust the door mirrors so that you can see a little of the car down the inside edge (the edge nearest the car). The road/pavement surface should be about a quarter the way up from the bottom. Having adjusted the mirrors, there will still be areas you cannot see – these are often called 'blind spots' or 'blind areas'. Your instructor will explain about these.

4. Seat belts

Fasten your seatbelt securely

Seat belts save lives and reduce the risk of serious injury. The law requires that all drivers and passengers (unless they have an exemption certificate) must wear a seat belt. As the driver you should encourage all of your passengers to wear their seat belts. If you are carrying passengers under 14 years of age, it is your responsibility to make sure they wear them.

Make sure there are no twists in the belt and that it lies flat across your chest and stomach. This will ensure that it works properly. When putting the belt on and taking it off, hold the buckle so that it doesn't fly up and hit you in the face or bang into the window.

5. Handbrake and neutral

You must make sure the car is secure and that it won't move when you switch on the engine. If your car is in gear or if the handbrake is not properly set, when you switch on the engine you could move unexpectedly.

Before turning the ignition key, check that the hand-brake (sometimes referred to as the parking brake) is on firmly. Make sure that it is raised to its highest position.

Now check that the gear lever is in the neutral position. (This is the position when no gear is engaged.) When you move the gear lever from side to side it should feel quite free.

How to start the engine

The starter or ignition switch is normally on or near the the steering column and usually combines an anti-theft steering lock.

As you turn the key, look for the battery charging and oil pressure warning lights. Check these go out when the engine starts.

Turn the key gently to operate the starter, when the engine starts release the key. To stop the engine turn the key back to its original position.

If the engine does not start, squeeze the accelerator (the pedal on the right) gently and try again. Do not pump the pedal as this can flood the engine and make starting even more difficult.

To start a cold engine, you may need to use the choke. This allows more fuel into the engine to make starting easier. However, this must be pushed in again as soon as the engine is warm. (Many cars have an automatic choke; check the vehicle handbook.)

If your car runs on diesel, you may have to wait until the warning light goes out before you can switch on the engine.

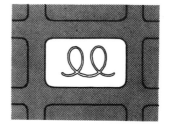

Using the handbrake

The handbrake is used to secure the car when you park it or are stationary for more than a few moments. It is also used to help you time moving off into gaps in the traffic.

You must make sure the car has stopped before applying the handbrake.

You must be able to apply and release the handbrake quickly, without looking down or wearing the ratchet mechanism (your instructor will explain this). Practise releasing and applying the handbrake while stationary.

First, press your footbrake (the middle pedal) firmly with your right foot. This will hold the car still while you practise.

To release the handbrake put your hand on to it with your thumb on the button, pull the lever up slightly and press the button in. Keep the button pressed in while you lower the handbrake.

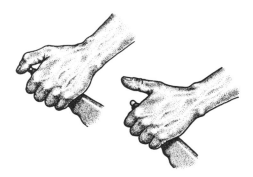

To put the handbrake on, press the button in and, keeping it in, pull the lever up firmly. Release the button to lock the brake on.

How to steer and operate the controls

Hold the wheel as in the diagram. Fold your palms loosely over the rim and rest your thumbs lightly up the flat of the wheel. Relax your shoulders and keep your arms free of your body.

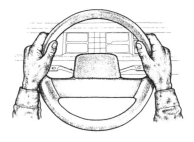

To steer accurately you should look well ahead at where you are going. You must be able to operate the main controls without looking at them. Looking down will result in your car wandering from side to side.

Try to keep both hands on the wheel when braking or cornering.

Operating switches

The most frequently used switches, such as the direction indicators, lights and windscreen wipers, are usually on the column just behind the steering wheel.

Practise using them with your fingertips, keeping your hands on the wheel.

Other important switches include the horn, windscreen washer and demisters. You can learn about these when you have mastered the main controls towards the end of Stage 4.

 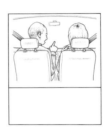 

Using the gears

The lower gears give you lots of pulling power and quick acceleration.

1st gear is used for moving off, manoeuvring and for creeping slowly in traffic and at junctions.

2nd gear is used for moving off down some steep hills, building up speed after moving away and driving at low speeds.

The higher gears allow you to drive comfortably at greater speeds. They are not so powerful and give less acceleration

3rd gear is used to build up speed and when you need more power for climbing hills. It also increases your control when going down steep hills and dealing with some bends.

4th is the gear used for driving at speeds generally higher than 30 mph, where there are no hazards to confront.

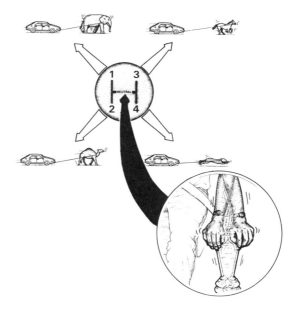

It is common to have four forward gears and one reverse. The neutral position allows the engine to run without turning the wheels. To check the gear lever is in neutral, move it from side to side.

Many cars have a 5th gear, which gives greater economy. This is normally only used on open roads when travelling constantly at higher speeds

How to change gear

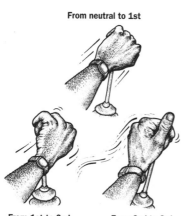

From neutral to 1st

From 1st to 2nd **From 2nd to 3rd**

When driving, you should be able to change gear without looking down at the lever. Practise this with the engine switched off and the clutch pressed down. Use a cupped palm to move the gear lever.

To practise finding 1st and 2nd, angle your palm and press the lever lightly away from you. Move it forward to 1st gear then straight back to 2nd.

To select 3rd and 4th gears angle the palm towards you. Move the lever gently from 2nd into 3rd and finally 4th.

Now move the lever back to 3rd, to 2nd and then to 1st. Keep practising until you have perfected these movements.

Finally practise changing from 4th to 2nd and 3rd to 1st.

Driving an automatic car

Learning to start, steer and stop is much easier in automatic cars. The right foot should normally be used to control the accelerator and footbrake. There is no clutch to operate and after the initial gear selection has been made, all subsequent changes are carried out automatically. They are regulated by the car's speed and the pressure applied on the accelerator by the driver.

In some automatic cars, the driver may engage a fixed low gear for carrying out low speed manoeuvres.

When driving an automatic car, the handbrake has to be used more often to avoid its natural tendency to creep forwards.

Automatic transmission enables drivers to concentrate on the more important things, such as planning ahead and steering. It makes learning to drive easier, particularly for older or disabled people. The exercises set out in Stage 4 are made much simpler but practice should still be carried out using the accelerator and the brake with the right foot.

Your instructor should explain about the extra use of the handbrake and the different techniques used to control the car at low speeds.

If you pass your test in an automatic car, you will only be entitled to drive this type of vehicle.

Using the accelerator and footbrake

Position your right foot so that it will pivot comfortably between the accelerator and brake pedals. To do this, cover the brake pedal with your right foot. Without looking down or moving your heel, practise pivoting between these pedals.

When you have found a comfortable position for your foot, get a feel for the brake pedal by pressing it lightly. The

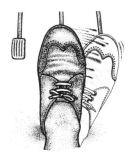

first pressure puts the brake lights on at the back of the car. When driving along, this will let anyone behind know you are slowing down. The harder you press the pedal, the more the car will slow down.

Now, start the engine. Remember your safety checks of: 'handbrake on and gear lever in neutral'.

Listen to the engine tickover speed and squeeze the accelerator gently until you hear a nice healthy purr. This is called setting the gas and you will need to do it when preparing to move off. Practise until you get it just right every time.

After moving off, you should notice that the car responds quite quickly to pressure on the accelerator when you are in the lower gears. Releasing the pressure will cause the car to slow down. This slowing effect is more pronounced in 1st and 2nd gears.

How the clutch works

The main purpose of the clutch is to connect and disconnect the power from the engine to the road wheels. It is needed so that changes can be made smoothly from one gear into another.

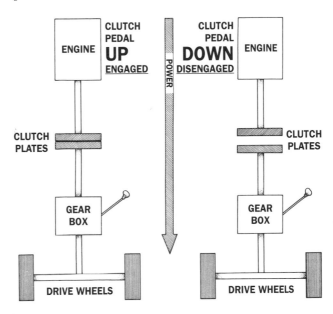

Using the clutch

To move off, change gear and stop, you should be able to use the clutch smoothly and without looking at your feet.

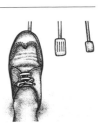

To begin with, cover the clutch with your left foot and then press it down. This will disconnect the engine from the gearbox. You will have to do this when changing gear and just before stopping.

Next let the pedal up smoothly. You will feel a powerful spring pushing your foot up.

Only a small part of the total pedal travel, known as the biting range, has any noticeable effect on the car. To move off and control very low speeds, you must be able to find the holding point at the bottom of this range.

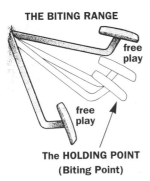

THE BITING RANGE

free play

free play

The HOLDING POINT
(Biting Point)

The holding point

The clutch consists of two friction plates that you must bring together smoothly when moving off. To do this you must first find the holding point. This allows the plates to touch lightly without driving the car. When the handbrake is released, and the clutch is at the holding point, the car should not move. This is known as a 'slipping clutch'. As the clutch is raised smoothly to the driving point it should creep at a very low speed.

The HOLDING POINT

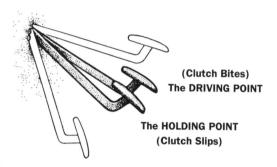

(Clutch Bites)
The DRIVING POINT

The HOLDING POINT
(Clutch Slips)

How to find the holding (biting) point

To practise finding the holding point you must first start the engine. Remember to make sure the handbrake is on and the gear lever in neutral. Now push the clutch down. Select 1st gear and set the gas by squeezing the accelerator slightly until you hear a nice healthy purr; this is about half as fast again as the engine tickover speed.

Raise the clutch pedal slowly by bending your ankle. Keeping your heel down will give you more support and positive clutch control. It may feel a little awkward at first, particularly if you have small feet or are in a car with high pedals. Padding under the carpet may help to overcome these problems.

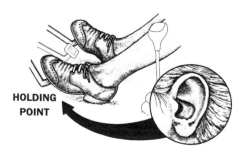

HOLDING POINT

As you raise the clutch, listen for a slight drop in the engine speed. When you hear or feel this, you have found the holding point and should keep the pedal still.

After keeping your foot still for a couple of seconds or so, push the clutch pedal down again and release the accelerator. Put the gear lever into neutral and relax your feet.

Practise this exercise until you can find the holding point fairly quickly every time.

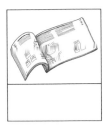 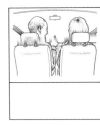 

Checkpoint

1 Getting into a suitable driving position will ensure you can:
   a. reach all the controls comfortably ✓
   b. use the controls properly
   c. lean against the head restraint
   d. see the road ahead clearly

2 Unless you have a medical exemption certificate, you must wear your seat belt:
   a. in towns or cities
   b. in rural areas
   c. when reversing
   d. on motorways

3 Head restraints provide protection against:
   a. neck and spinal injuries ✓
   b. the effects of whiplash
   c. severe headaches
   d. fatigue on long journeys

4 You should check your seat position:
   a. as soon as you drive away
   b. if someone else has been driving
   c. before you switch on the engine ✓
   d. when you have been driving for about five minutes

5 When driving, you should:
   a. never take a hand off the wheel
   b. never take both hands off the wheel ✓
   c. look where you want the car to go
   d. let the wheel spin back after turning

6   You should avoid:
    a.   applying the handbrake before the car has stopped
    ✓b.   applying the handbrake after the car has stopped
    c.   releasing the handbrake until the car is moving
    d.   releasing the handbrake until you have checked it's
         safe to move

7   In an automatic vehicle, you should:
    a.   use the handbrake only when parking
    b.   apply the footbrake before engaging 'drive'
    ✓c.   use the handbrake more frequently
    d.   use the handbrake less frequently

8   Before starting the engine check:
    a.   your door is properly closed
    b.   all doors are properly closed
    c.   your seat and mirrors are adjusted
    ✓d.   the handbrake is on

9   You should understand the function of those controls
    which have a bearing on road safety. These include the:
    ✓a.   indicators
    b.   mobile phone
    c.   radio
    d.   lights
    e.   demisters

10   Most interior mirrors have flat glass. This:
    a.   gives a distorted picture
    ✓b.   gives a true picture
    c.   makes it easier to judge the speed and distance of
         following traffic
    d.   makes it difficult to judge the speed and distance of
         following traffic

11   Most exterior mirrors have convex glass. This:
    ✓a.   gives a wider field of vision
    b.   makes things behind seem larger
    c.   makes things behind seem smaller
    d.   makes them seem to be nearer
    e.   makes them seem to be further away

12   You get a truer picture from:
    a.   the interior mirror
    b.   the nearside door mirror
    c.   the offside door mirror
    ✓d.   your blind spot checks

13 Blind spots should be checked:
    a. before moving off
    b. changing lanes
    c. joining a motorway
    d. before checking the mirrors
    e. after moving off

14 In an automatic car, the:
    a. left foot operates the brake only
    b. right foot operates the accelerator only
    c. right foot operates both pedals
    d. left foot operates the clutch only

15 Starting the engine while in gear may:
    a. cause the car to move
    b. damage the handbrake
    c. save fuel
    d. cause the engine to stall

16 The clutch:
    a. transmits power to the gearbox
    b. disconnects power from the gearbox
    c. controls the speed of the engine
    d. helps when coasting

17 Door mirrors:
    a. help reduce blind spots to the sides
    b. completely overcome all blind spots
    c. need only be used by experienced drivers
    d. need only be used when reversing

18 In a manual car, the left foot operates the:
    a. brake and clutch pedals
    b. brake pedal only
    c. clutch only
    d. accelerator only

19 In a manual car, the right foot operates the:
    a. clutch and brake pedals
    b. accelerator only
    c. accelerator and brake pedals
    d. brake pedal only

20 The choke is used for:
    a. starting a cold engine
    b. cooling down a hot engine
    c. increasing the flow of fuel
    d. increasing the air flow

21 Direction indicators should be operated:
    a. without releasing the steering wheel
    b. only when the wheel is released
    c. by either hand according to the direction required
    d. by the instructor in the early stages

22 The handbrake should be used:
    a. every time you stop the car
    b. when you are stopped for more than a few moments
    c. only when you are parking your car
    d. whenever you stop at 'stop' signs

23 When neutral is engaged, the engine is:
    a. disconnected from the road wheels
    b. connected to the road wheels
    c. ticking over at a very high rate
    d. slowing the car down

24 1st gear is the:
    a. least powerful gear
    b. most powerful gear
    c. most economical gear
    d. one used when driving at high speeds

25 Keep both hands on the steering wheel:
    a. when braking
    b. at all times
    c. when cornering
    d. only for driving in straight lines

26 'Tickover' is:
    a. the engine's normal running speed
    b. achieved by smooth acceleration
    c. when you are not accelerating
    d. the timing of the engine's clock

27 'Setting the gas' means the engine is:
    a. running faster than tickover
    b. running more slowly than tickover
    c. switching on the ignition
    d. finding the 'biting point'

28 The footbrake should be used:
    a. gently and progressively
    b. in good time
    c. firmly and quickly
    d. harshly in emergencies

29 Coasting means you could be:
   a. put in danger
   b. making more economical use of fuel
   c. out of control
   d. going faster than you want to

30 Looking down at the gear lever will:
   a. cause you to wander off course
   b. affect your concentration
   c. help you avoid selecting the wrong gear
   d. help you select the correct gear

You will find the answers on page 221

Scores: 1st try ☐ ; 2nd try ☐ ; 3rd try ☐

Record your scores in the appendix on page 225.

Starting to drive

Introduction

During this stage you will be learning how to move off, change gear, steer and stop the car. Make sure that you can carry out all of these skills reasonably well before going out to practise. Your instructor will advise you when you are ready to go out with someone else.

It is important that you learn the basic procedures in very quiet areas. Housing estates with lots of parked vehicles and other hazards are not really suitable.

Your instructor will talk you through each exercise until you can manage on your own. Directions will be given in plenty of time to allow you carry out all of the individual skills without rushing. However, because of lack of experience with learners, you may find that you are not given enough time by someone else. If you find yourself becoming confused and rushed, ask your supervisor to give instructions much earlier.

Avoid talking while you are practising – this will only distract you. Concentrate, keep your eyes on the road and listen carefully to directions. The following are useful instructions:

- I would like you to take the next road on the right.

- Take the second road on the right, this is the first one.

- At the end of the road, turn left please.

Learn **Highway Code** rules:

135–137 Moving off and the normal driving position
213–219 Parking.

Read **The Driving Test** pages 27, 28, 29 and 38.

 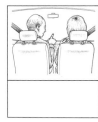 

It's never too soon for you to start getting into the mirror–signal–manoeuvre routine.

Using the mirror

You should check the mirrors well before signalling and making any changes in your speed or direction. Check them before moving off, accelerating, pulling out to pass parked cars, overtaking, positioning to turn, and slowing down or stopping.

Using your mirrors properly will enable you to act on what you see in them. Your instructor should teach you how to do this.

Giving signals

You should give a signal if it will help to warn or inform any other road user of your intentions. The signals you will mainly be using at this stage are the brake lights and direction indicators.

The red brake lights at the rear of your car will come on automatically when you press the footbrake. They tell drivers behind that you are slowing down. If you see brake lights on a vehicle ahead you should check your mirror and start easing off the accelerator in preparation for braking.

Indicator lights flash at the front and rear of your car to let others know that you intend to change direction or stop. Signals should be given in plenty of time so that others may respond to them.

Making a manoeuvre

'Manoeuvre' is the word used to describe any change that you make in your position or speed. It also involves continually looking and assessing what's happening around you so that your actions don't affect anyone else.

How to move off

You should normally use 1st gear for moving off except when pulling away down a steep hill.

Get ready to move: take an initial look to the front and in the mirrors for traffic and pedestrians and then get ready to move.

To prepare to move, push the clutch down and select 1st gear. Find the holding point and keep the clutch still.

Check it's safe to move: by looking in the interior and door mirrors. To be 100 per cent sure, look around for other road users in your blind areas. Be prepared to wait. Decide if you need to signal. This should be given if it will help to warn or inform others that you intend moving away. Be careful, however, not to use a signal which may confuse drivers coming up behind you.

To move away: have the handbrake ready to release. You must be sure it's safe before letting your car move by checking your blind area again. You can time the moment for moving with the release of the handbrake. This should allow the car to creep forwards. If the car doesn't move, let the clutch up a little more.

To increase speed, press the accelerator gently and when the car is moving, start easing the clutch up slowly. Continue to press the accelerator gently as you raise the clutch smoothly to the top.

You will need to change into 2nd gear soon after moving off.

To change gear

1st gear provided the power you needed for pulling the weight of the car away. You don't need so much power now so you need to change into 2nd. This will allow you to accelerate from the low speed. Remember, when selecting 1st and 2nd gears, to angle your palm away from you.

Preparing to change (from 1st to 2nd): grip the wheel a little more firmly with your right hand and, keeping your eyes on the road, cup your hand over the gear lever ready. Cover the clutch without touching it.

From 1st to 2nd   **From 2nd to 3rd**

To change gear (from 1st to 2nd): push the clutch down quickly and take your foot off the gas pedal at the same time. Using gentle pressure, move the gear lever from 1st into 2nd.

Raise the clutch smoothly to the top and then press the accelerator gently to increase the engine speed.

Put your left hand back on to the wheel.

After accelerating in 2nd to between 15 and 25 to 20 mph, change to 3rd. Use this gear to build up speed to about 25 to 30mph, then change into 4th. For 3rd and 4th gears, remember to angle your palm towards you.

It is inadvisable to drive for prolonged periods with the clutch covered. Practise placing your left foot on the floor away from the pedal after each change.

 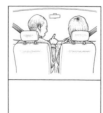 

How to steer and judge your driving position

You are likely to drift towards things you look at. Look well ahead to where you want the car to go.

Don't look at the kerb or the road just in front of the bonnet. Avoid staring at nearby objects, it will only make you steer towards them. Try to drive about a metre (2 to 3 feet) out from the kerb and look in the direction you want the car to go. Plan your course well ahead by memorizing the position of any obstructions. Rely on your side vision to sense your position in the road and to judge the clearance you are leaving between your car and parked vehicles. Look ahead at the space at the side and in front of the obstruction – this will help you to give enough clearance.

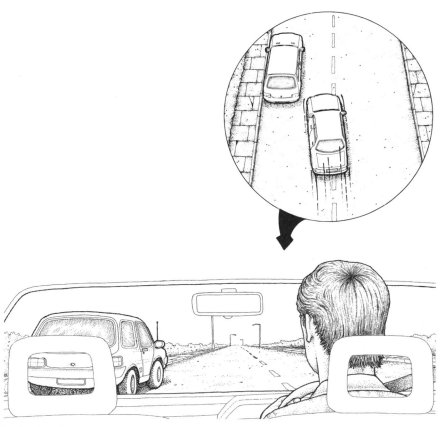

Look ahead to judge clearance

How to steer and drive at a safe speed

Look into the distance for road signs or obstructions and be prepared to slow down well before reaching any bends or junctions.

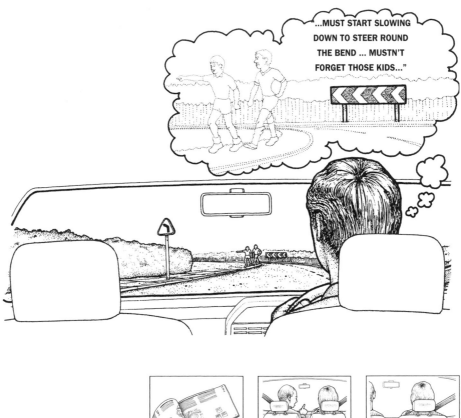

"...MUST START SLOWING DOWN TO STEER ROUND THE BEND ... MUSTN'T FORGET THOSE KIDS..."

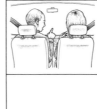

Stopping and parking

Try to park well away from bends, junctions and hilltops. These are all places where the driver's view is already restricted.

Parking your car in an unsafe place will increase the danger by forcing others on to the wrong side of the road when they can't see approaching traffic and approaching drivers can't see them.

Do not park dangerously

Find a straight part of the road and, putting the mirror–signal–manoeuvre routine into practice, stop as close to the kerb as you can without touching it.

Look ahead to judge clearance

First of all, check for following traffic and, if necessary, signal to tell them what you are going to do (ie, give a left signal).

The secret of stopping smoothly is to brake early. Brake gently at first, gradually building up into a firm pressure until you feel the car slowing down slightly more than you think is necessary. Gradually ease some pressure from the brake to let the car roll gently to a stop. Keep both hands on the wheel while you are braking.

Remember to push the clutch down just before you stop and keep it down until you have applied the hand-brake and put the gear lever into neutral. Rest your feet and switch off the engine.

Before you open the door to get out of the car, look round for other road users who may be hidden in the blind areas.

How to stop within the distance you can see is clear

Look, and be ready to slow down, for other road users who might move into the road or turn across your path. Watch out for people and vehicles moving from behind obstructions.

Steering and speed anticipate sudden movements into the road

Checkpoint

1   The term 'set the gas' refers to the:
   a.   accelerator and engine speed
   b.   clutch and its biting range
   c.   ignition switch
   d.   use of liquid propane gas (LPG)

2   To prepare for moving off, you should:
   a.   select 1st and push down the clutch
   b.   push down the clutch and select 1st
   c.   set the gas and push down the clutch
   d.   cover the brake and clutch pedals

3   To find the 'holding point', you should:
   a.   listen to the engine speed
   b.   look down at your feet
   c.   feel the vibration of the gear lever
   d.   keep your right foot on the brake

4   You can control the clutch smoothly by:
   a.   lowering the engine speed
   b.   raising the engine speed
   c.   listening carefully for 'biting point'
   d.   keeping your left heel down

5   Before moving off from the left on a level road, you should:
   a.   check the interior mirror
   b.   check the offside door mirror
   c.   look over your right shoulder
   d.   release the footbrake

6   For moving off you should:
   a.   always use 1st gear
   b.   normally use 1st gear
   c.   use 2nd gear for some down slopes
   d.   never use 2nd gear

7 When preparing to change gear:
   a. look at the gear lever
   b. put your hand to the gear lever ready
   c. cover the clutch
   d. cover the brake

8 To move the gear lever smoothly:
   a. 'palm' your hand towards the position of the gear you need
   b. grip the lever as tightly as you can
   c. push the lever as quickly as you can
   d. allow the clutch to come up during the gear change

9 To steer accurately you should look:
   a. well ahead at where you want the car to go
   b. towards the kerb to help guide you
   c. at the central white line
   d. at the road surface just ahead of the bonnet

10 When driving along a straight road you should steer:
   a. about a metre away from the kerb
   b. as close to the kerb as you can
   c. about a metre from the centre line
   d. with your hands at 'twenty-to-four'

11 Parking near bends and hill crests:
   a. is inconsiderate
   b. is dangerous
   c. puts others at risk
   d. is only advisable on multi-lane roads

12 The correct sequence for approaching hazards is:
   a. signal–manoeuvre–mirror
   b. mirror–signal–manoeuvre
   c. signal–mirror–manoeuvre
   d. manoeuvre–mirror–signal

13 Brake lights come on when the:
   a. indicators are switched on
   b. footbrake is pressed
   c. accelerator is released
   d. handbrake is applied

14 To stop smoothly and accurately, you should:
   a. brake gently and early
   b. keep both hands on the wheel

    c. look towards the kerb
    d. ease the brake pressure just as you are stopping

15 Before leaving your car, you should:
    a. apply the handbrake
    b. switch off the engine
    c. select neutral
    d. switch on the hazard lights

16 The correct sequence for braking is:
    a. hard–gently–firm
    b. gently–firm–hard
    c. gently–firm–gently
    d. hard–gently–handbrake

17 If you park near junctions, you will:
    a. make other drivers' observations more difficult
    b. make it difficult for pedestrians to cross the road
    c. cause danger and inconvenience
    d. make it easier for yourself to move off again

18 Before moving off you should:
    a. use all of the mirrors
    b. look around to check the blind spots
    c. always use a signal
    d. use a signal if necessary

19 Once on the move, you should:
    a. drive half a metre out from the kerb
    b. keep well over to the right on right hand bends
    c. keep well over to the left on right hand bends
    d. drive as close to the centre line as you think is safe

20 Before reaching a long downhill slope you should:
    a. push down the clutch
    b. use the brakes firmly to control your speed
    c. select a lower gear
    d. select a higher gear

21 Smaller vehicles are difficult to see. Look out particularly for:
    a. cycles
    b. motorcycles
    c. minibuses
    d. small goods vehicles

22 You may move off:
    a. as soon as you have checked the mirrors
    b. as soon as you have signalled
    c. the moment you release the handbrake
    d. only when you are sure it is safe

23 You must not wait or park where there are restrictions:
    a. shown by yellow lines
    b. shown by school entrance markings
    c. unless you have permission from a school crossing operator
    d. unless you use hazard warning flashers

24 If you have to stop at the road side you should:
    a. switch off all lights
    b. ensure you don't hit anyone with your door
    c. get passengers out by the kerb side
    d. always park on the left

25 The Highway Code lists some areas which have parking spaces reserved for specific road users. These include:
    a. learner drivers
    b. elderly drivers
    c. orange badgeholders
    d. residents

26 Parking on the pavement can inconvenience:
    a. other drivers
    b. people in wheelchairs
    c. people with prams
    d. the visually impaired

27 You should not park:
    a. where you would prevent access for emergency vehicles.
    b. further than 10 metres away from any junctions
    c. within 20 metres of any junctions
    d. where it would force others to enter a cycle lane

28 Other places where you should not park include:
    a. in front of entrances to property
    b. bus lanes during their hours of operation
    c. roads with a single centre line which is broken
    d. roads marked with red lines

29 You should not stop on an urban clearway:
    a. at any time
    b. during its hours of operation
    c. without lights
    d. unless picking up or setting down passengers

30 You must leave pedestrian crossings clear:
    a. at all times
    b. unless in a traffic queue
    c. unless waiting to turn right
    d. during the hours of daylight only

You will find the answers on page 222

Scores: 1st try [   ] ; 2nd try [   ] ; 3rd try [   ] .

Record your scores in the appendix on page 225.

Moving off, driving along and stopping

Introduction

Up to now your driving instructor should have been telling you everything you needed to do. This should have helped you 'get things right first time' and to build up your confidence.

Having lots of practise at the exercises in this stage should help improve your control skills and give you the confidence to start doing more for yourself. The better you are at controlling your car the easier it will be when you have to deal with hazards and other traffic.

When you can control the car with confidence, you can start practising the manoeuvres in Stage 6.

During your driving lessons, your ADI will be checking all around to make sure that everything you do is safe and is not affecting others. When you are practising privately, ask your supervisor to do the same.

The following is your reading list before going out to practise:

Read **The Driving Manual** – Part 5: Starting to Drive.
Read **The Driving Test** – pages 29–33.
Learn the following **Highway Code** rules:

85–92	Signals
97–102	Braking
105	Stopping distances

Exercise 1 – How to control the car at low speeds and move off smoothly

Practise each step of this exercise on a fairly wide road. Find a safe position on a slight uphill slope and stop about a foot away from the kerb. Practise each step until you can carry it out smoothly with the car under control.

Step 1 – Finding the holding point

With the engine running, select 1st gear, set the gas and find the holding point. If there are no other road users nearby, release the handbrake. Keep your feet still and hold the car stationary for two or three seconds.

If the car moves forwards, press the clutch down a little. If it rolls back, keep calm and raise the clutch slightly.

Finding the biting point

Step 2 – Moving off slowly with a slipping clutch

Follow the procedure in Step 1 and then raise the clutch slightly until the car moves forwards.

Now press the clutch down slightly and try to creep forwards very slowly without stopping.

Step 3 – How to regain control when rolling backwards

Over-anxiety about rolling back can be a major cause of loss of control on uphill junctions. This exercise should help to increase your confidence by showing how easy it is to regain control and stop the car rolling.

Follow the procedure in Step 1 and then push the clutch down slightly until the car starts rolling backwards. Let it roll for two or three yards. To regain control, raise the clutch gradually until you can feel the car stopping.

It is important to control the clutch very gently. If you let the pedal up too far or too quickly it may stall the engine or cause the car to jump forwards. At junctions this could be more dangerous than rolling back a little.

Step 4 – How to move off efficiently

Remember to check the 'blind areas' before moving off. Follow the procedures in Steps 1 and 2 until the car is creeping forwards.

To accelerate and move away efficiently you should start gently pressing the accelerator and then slowly raise the clutch. Continue accelerating gently as you let the clutch up.

If the car jerks, you need to let the clutch up more slowly or press the accelerator a little more. If the engine roars, use less pressure on the accelerator or let the clutch up a little further.

Remember to change into 2nd gear as soon as possible after moving off.

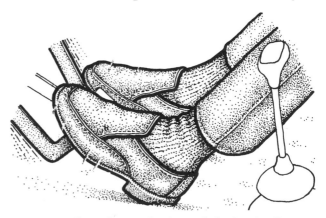

Gently press down the accelerator and slowly raise the clutch

Exercise 2 – How to control low speeds when moving away downhill

When moving off downhill there are times, such as in heavy traffic, at junctions, or when moving out from behind parked vehicles, when you will need to restrain the speed and move off very slowly. To do this you must keep the clutch just below the holding point and use the footbrake to prevent the car rolling away too quickly.

To practise, park on a quiet road facing downhill. Select 1st gear, or 2nd if on a steep slope. Apply the footbrake to hold the car and release the handbrake.

If there are no road users nearby, raise the clutch to just below the holding point. You will have to 'feel' for this as the change in the engine note will be less noticeable. Gradually ease the footbrake off to let the car roll slowly forwards. Raise the clutch smoothly all the way to the top and gently accelerate away.

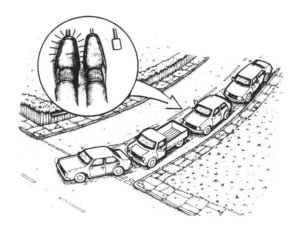

Exercise 3 – Learning to accelerate and change up through the gears

Practise this exercise on a fairly straight, wide road where there is little or no other traffic.

Move off and change into 2nd gear as soon as you can. Accelerate to about 15–20 mph, then change into 3rd gear. Accelerate in 3rd to 25–30 mph and then change into 4th.

After completing the exercise, find a safe position and park at the side of the road. Discuss your performance with your supervisor to find out where you can improve. Practise until you feel confident about changing up through the gears on your own.

Exercise 4 – Learning to brake and change down through the gears

To practise this exercise you will need to move off and build your speed up until you are driving at about 30 mph in 4th gear. Your supervisor should help by keeping a look out, making sure it is safe for you to carry out each step of the exercise.

Step 1 – Changing down through the gears

Check the mirror to make sure it is safe. Brake gently to slow the car down to about 20 mph. Release the brake and change into 3rd gear. Check the mirror again and, if safe, reapply the brake gently and slow down to about 10 mph. Release the brake and change into 2nd gear.

Check the mirror and, if safe, build up your speed, changing up through the gears, until you are travelling at about 30 mph again. Keep practising the exercise until you feel confident.

Step 2 – Changing from 4th into 2nd gear

Move off and build up your speed until you are travelling at about 30 mph in 4th gear. Check the mirror to make sure it is safe and brake gently to slow the car down to about 10 mph. Release the brake and change from 4th gear into 2nd.

If safe, build up your speed, changing up through the gears, until you reach about 30 mph again. Keep practising until you can carry out the exercise smoothly and confidently.

Step 3 – Changing from 3rd to 1st gear

To practise this exercise you will need to move off and build up your speed until you are driving along at about 20 mph in 3rd gear.

If safe, brake gently to slow the car down until you have almost stopped. Push the clutch down, keep it down and release the brake so the car keeps rolling forwards very slowly. Just before the car stops, change from 3rd gear into 1st.

When safe, move off again and accelerate, changing up through the gears until you reach about 20 mph in 3rd so that you can practise again. Keep practising the exercise until you feel confident.

Exercise 5 – How to stop smoothly at a given point

To practise this exercise you must find a fairly straight quiet road with plenty of distinctive features such as telegraph poles, or trees. The object will be to stop with your front bumper level with one of these. You will need lots of practice so that you can consistently bring the car to a smooth stop at the required place.

When safe, move off and build up your speed to about 25–30 mph with 3rd or 4th gear selected. Your supervisor should look ahead and select your stopping place. Check your mirror and, when safe, cover the brake. This will have a slight braking effect as the engine begins to slow down. Use this to help you judge how much braking pressure you will need. To begin with, squeeze the brake very gently. Gradually press it harder until you appear to be stopping short of the required position.

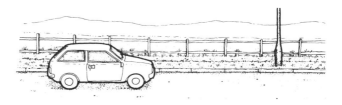

Gradually ease the braking pressure and push the clutch down. This will allow the car to roll up to the stopping point. Select 1st gear ready for moving away.

As the car comes to a rest with the front almost level with the stopping point, set the gas and find the holding point. Take care not to let the clutch up too far. Hold the car still for a second or two while checking it is safe to move away.

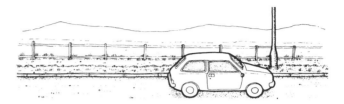

Exercise 6 – How to stop in an emergency

Anticipation helps you to avoid emergencies. You will learn more about this in Stage 8.

For now all you need to know is that the earlier you spot any possible danger, the sooner you can act on it. Taking early precautions, such as slowing down, will reduce the likelihood of needing to brake hard at the last moment.

Slow down early to reduce sudden braking

Even experienced drivers sometimes find themselves having to stop quickly because they have failed to anticipate danger, or something completely unexpected happens.

Make sure **you** can stop quickly before you go into heavy traffic.

Practise the emergency stop on a quiet, fairly wide and straight road.

Before you move away your supervisor **must** demonstrate the signal to be given for the stop and, after moving away, ensure there are no other road users about before giving it.

In a real emergency there is little time to use the mirrors before braking. Make sure you are using them often as you drive along so that you are aware of what is happening behind.

Step 1 – Braking firmly to a stop

Your first attempts at stopping quickly should be carried out at fairly low speeds. Just practise stopping with a little more than the pressure needed for a normal stop.

When the signal to stop is given, respond at once and pivot quickly to the brake. Press the brake firmly but progressively and keep a firm hold of the wheel with both hands. Wait until the car has nearly stopped before pushing the clutch down. Pushing it down too soon can increase the stopping distance and the risk of skidding. After coming to a complete stop, put the handbrake on.

Remember you were in your normal driving position on the road before you stopped. Before moving away, check that it is safe all around the car.

Step 2 – Stopping quickly as in an emergency

Repeat the previous exercise, gradually increasing the speed and the braking pressure until you can stop the car quickly, and without skidding or swerving. It may feel as if your car travelled a long way before coming to a stop. Read about stopping distances in your Highway Code and remember that in wet conditions these will be much longer. Use a lighter pressure on the brake or you may lock the wheels and skid.

Exercise 7 – Steering practice and checking the instruments

Step 1 – Anticipating when to turn the wheel

Find a quiet road with some sharp bends.

When approaching left bends, move your left hand towards the top of the wheel ready to pull it down to steer round the curve in the road.

When approaching right bends, move your right hand towards the top of the wheel ready to pull it down to steer round the curve in the road.

Step 2 – Steering with one hand

Although you should keep both hands on the wheel as much as possible, there are times when you need to change gear or operate the lights, wipers and other controls.

Find a straight, quiet road where you can steer with one hand while you practise using these controls. You can also practise opening and closing the windows.

Step 3 – Giving arm signals

Practise giving arm signals for left and right turns and for slowing down.

Step 4 – When to check the instruments

The instruments help to keep you informed of the condition of your car. Ignoring warning lights can result in breakdowns or serious damage.

When checking them, look well ahead and glance quickly at one instrument at a time. Only do this when there is nothing much happening on the road and you can spare the time.

You should stop and get help if the brake warning light comes on; if the temperature gauge shows the engine is overheating; or if the oil pressure is low.

Find out from your car's handbook what all of the symbols on the dashboard mean.

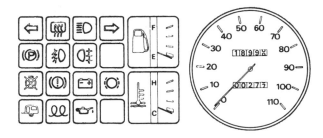

Checkpoint

1 At 30 mph your thinking distance is:
 a. 9 m (30 ft)
 b. 14 m (45 ft)
 c. 18 m (60 ft)
 d. 21 m (70 ft)

2 At 30 mph your braking distance is:
 a. 9 m (30 ft)
 b. 14 m (45 ft)
 c. 18 m (60 ft)
 d. 23 m (75 ft)

3 At 30 mph your overall stopping distance is:
 a. 9 m (30 ft)
 b. 14 m (45 ft)
 c. 18 m (60 ft)
 d. 23 m (75 ft)

4 At 40 mph your overall stopping distance is:
 a. 23 m (75 ft)
 b. 36 m (120 ft)
 c. 55 m (180 ft)
 d. 73 m (240 ft)

5 At 70 mph your overall stopping distance is:
 a. 38 m (125 ft)
 b. 53 m (175 ft)
 c. 75 m (245 ft)
 d. 96 m (315 ft)

6 Signs giving orders are normally:
 a. rectangular
 b. triangular
 c. circular
 d. hexagonal

7 On wet roads, the gap between you and the vehicle ahead should:
a. remain the same
b. be halved
c. be at least doubled
d. be two seconds

8 In an emergency you should:
a. brake gently and quickly
b. brake immediately
c. harshly and gradually
d. try to lock the wheels

9 An ABS system should:
a. prevent skidding
b. help maintain steering control
c. help with braking at all times
d. not make you alter your braking

10 Brake lights mean the driver:
a. is slowing down
b. intends to slow down
c. is warning following drivers
d. intends to stop

11 A solid white line across the end of a road means you must:
a. stop at the line
b. not park in that road
c. go if the way is clear
d. apply the handbrake

12 Double broken lines across the end of a road mean:
a. stop before you reach the line
b. stop at the line
c. give way to traffic in the major road
d. go if the way is clear

13 Double solid lines along the centre of the road mean:
a. do not overtake
b. do not cross the lines
c. cross the lines only when you can see the road is clear
d. cross the lines only to pass a slow vehicle

14 Long white lines in the centre of the road mean:
a. there is a hazard ahead
b. you must not cross the line
c. you may overtake if it is safe
d. you must not overtake

15 To stop in the shortest possible distance, you should brake:
a. as hard as you can with the clutch down
b. until the wheels lock up
c. firmly and push the clutch down just before you stop
d. gently and then as hard as possible

16 Braking in an emergency you should:
a. keep both hands on the wheel
b. brake hard and change down a gear
c. brake but do not touch the clutch
d. brake firmly and push the clutch down at the last moment

17 Not keeping regular checks on the instruments may result in:
a. breakdowns
b. damage
c. your becoming disorientated
d. not being aware of your speed

18 If there are solid double white lines in the centre of the road, you may overtake:
a. only if the road ahead is clear
b. to pass a stationary vehicle
c. to enter property
d. to pass a road maintenance vehicle travelling at less than 10 mph

19 Areas of white diagonal stripes on the road are to:
a. separate the traffic lanes
b. help speed up the traffic flow
c. protect right turning traffic
d. show you where to position

20 You should drive at a speed:
a. dictated by the road signs
b. so you can stop in the distance you can see is clear
c. dictated by the road conditions
d. to keep up with the other drivers

21 Speed limits are maximums. You should reduce your speed when:
   a. there are no hazards ahead
   b. weather conditions make it safer to do so
   c. driving at night
   d. sharing the road with motorcyclists

22 Coasting is travelling in neutral or with the clutch down. It means:
   a. engine braking is eliminated
   b. your speed downhill can increase quickly
   c. you will achieve more fuel economy
   d. the appropriate gear may be more difficult to select

23 If you have to drive through water, your brakes may be less effective. After driving through, you should:
   a. brake hard to dry out the brakes
   b. keep the clutch down longer
   c. push the brake gently to make sure they work
   d. gently apply light pressure when driving slowly

24 When slowing down to a stop you should:
   a. brake early and lightly
   b. brake more firmly as you begin to stop
   c. put more pressure on as the car comes to rest
   d. ease the pressure off as the car comes to rest

25 Skids are caused by the driver:
   a. planning too far ahead
   b. driving too fast for the conditions
   c. steering too harshly
   d. accelerating harshly

26 Signals should be used·
   a. to inform others of your intentions
   b. clearly and in good time
   c. for changing course or direction
   d. to inform people of what you have done

27 Arm signals are useful when:
   a. stopping at stop signs
   b. reinforcing indicator signals
   c. stopping at pedestrian crossings
   d. informing pedestrians

28 When you see other drivers signalling you should:
   a. wait until you are sure of what they are doing
   b. assume they will act on the signal
   c. proceed if they are flashing at you
   d. be aware their signal may not have been cancelled

29 A broken centre line on your side means:
   a. it is safe to overtake
   b. there are no hazards ahead
   c. you may park at certain times
   d. you may cross the line only if safe

30 Always use the mirrors before:
   a. moving off
   b. changing direction
   c. signalling
   d. slowing down
   e. accelerating

You will find the answers on page 222

Scores: 1st try [ ] ; 2nd try [ ] ; 3rd try [ ]

Record your scores in the appendix on page 225.

Gaining confidence as you drive

Introduction

Practise in a quiet area with fairly wide roads, rounded corners and not too many parked cars.

To begin with, learn how to apply the mirror–signal–manoeuvre (MSM) routine for turning left and right into side roads. Practise until you feel confident that you can follow the procedures.

When you have mastered these exercises, practise the MSM routine for approaching and emerging from the end of roads. To begin with you should practise at junctions where you will have a clear view into the main road.

When you can cope confidently with the simpler junctions, progress to those with sharper corners and roads with a little more traffic. However, you should still avoid very busy junctions and those on steep uphill gradients.

Don't attempt too much too soon. If things go wrong it will shatter your confidence. Your supervisor must be sure you can cope before taking you on very busy roads, at junctions on hills and those where your view is restricted.

Before practising, read **The Driving Test**, page 38. Learn the following **Highway Code** rules:

103–104	Speed limits
106–111	Lines and markings on the road
122–124	General advice
130	Driving in built up areas
135–139	Moving off and driving along
146–148	Road junctions
155–156	Turning right
158–159	Turning left

Work through this section of the book and complete the checkpoint before going out in the car. Match your answers with those given on page 221. Revise anything you feel doubtful about.

More about the mirror–signal–manoeuvre routine

Get into the habit of beginning the mirror–signal–manoeuvre routine early when approaching junctions and other hazards such as obstructions in the road. When you look in the mirror, try to judge the speed and position of vehicles behind. In the early stages, your instructor/supervisor should help you to judge whether your manoeuvre will be safe. Decide whether a signal will help to warn or inform others about your actions. Allow time for them to see and respond to your signals.

A manoeuvre is any action involving a change to your speed or position.

Positioning your car early helps to confirm your signals and intentions. The correct position provides you with the maximum view and safety margins. Others can see you, you can see them and your view of any possible danger is improved.

Try to get your car into position well before you reach a turn or other hazard. This will cause the least inconvenience to the flow of traffic.

Approach junctions and other hazards slowly enough to look for a safe opportunity to proceed. To do this, you will need to slow down before reaching the junction giving you time to select a lower gear ready to accelerate away.

Remember, the brakes are for slowing – the gears for going. Slow down before changing down. If you need to change gear, do it as you finish braking or after you have released the footbrake.

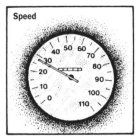

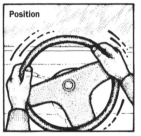

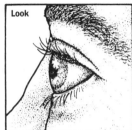

Approaching hazards too fast will result in frequent and unnecessary stops because you won't have time to look properly on the approach.

Start looking early as you approach a junction. Make sure you can see properly before deciding to go forward.

Using the MSM routine at junctions

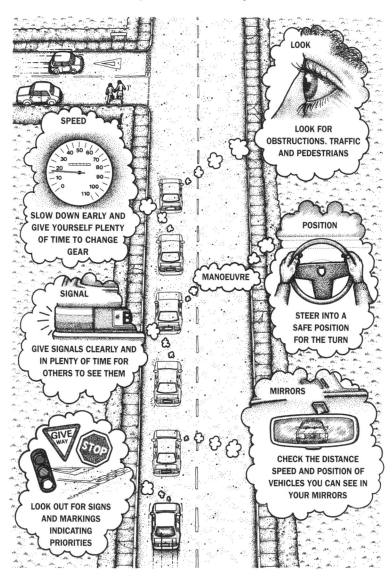

LOOK

LOOK FOR OBSTRUCTIONS. TRAFFIC AND PEDESTRIANS

SPEED

SLOW DOWN EARLY AND GIVE YOURSELF PLENTY OF TIME TO CHANGE GEAR

POSITION

STEER INTO A SAFE POSITION FOR THE TURN

MANOEUVRE

SIGNAL

GIVE SIGNALS CLEARLY AND IN PLENTY OF TIME FOR OTHERS TO SEE THEM

MIRRORS

CHECK THE DISTANCE SPEED AND POSITION OF VEHICLES YOU CAN SEE IN YOUR MIRRORS

GIVE WAY

STOP

LOOK OUT FOR SIGNS AND MARKINGS INDICATING PRIORITIES

Positioning your car correctly

For normal driving, and before turning left, position the car about a metre (3 feet) from the kerb. Before turning right, position the car just to the left of the centre of the road.

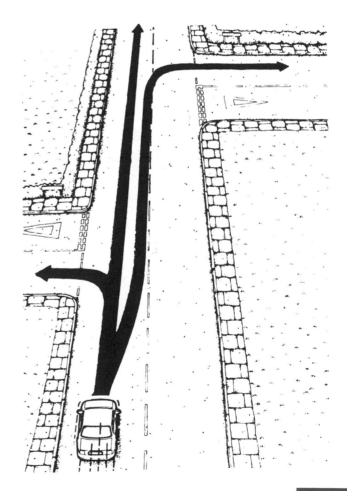

Be ready to give way to pedestrians

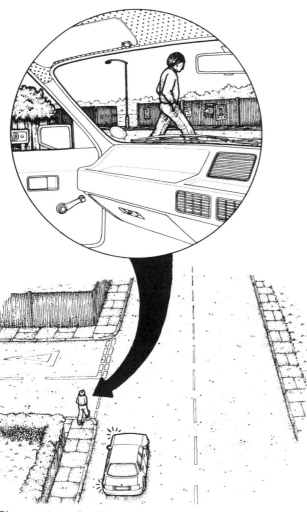

Give way to pedestrians crossing any road you are turning into. Watch out particularly for those with their back to you. They may not have seen or heard you and could walk into the road without looking. In some instances, where they are walking towards the road, it may be appropriate to sound the horn lightly.

Give way to pedestrians

How to turn corners

Before taking a hand from the wheel to change gear or use other controls, take a firmer grip with the other hand. Just before reaching a bend or corner, slide the right hand when turning right, or the left hand when turning left, towards the top of the wheel ready to pull it down.

For accurate positioning and steering, it is more important for you to concentrate on where you want to go than on what your hands are doing. Look well ahead into the new road.

Dangers to avoid when turning left

When turning left it is important for you to maintain a position about a metre from the kerb.

If you get too close to the kerb, the rear wheel may cut in and strike it. This could damage the tyre leading to a puncture or result in it becoming illegal to use.

Positioning too close to the kerb may also cause you to swing out into the path of others approaching the end of the road.

Swinging out

Driving too close to the kerb and swinging out just before you turn could cause following drivers to swerve across the road to pass you.

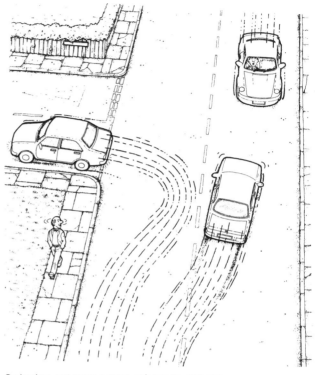

Swinging out may cause others to swerve

Positioning your car for turning right

The point of turn

The main danger when turning right is from oncoming traffic. You must normally let approaching vehicles go first. Slow down and hold back until they have passed the junction. If you reach the point of turn first, stop and wait just short of it.

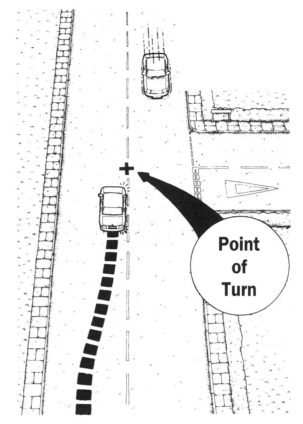

The point of turn

Position before turning right

Get into position early and maintain it. On a wide road this normally allows following vehicles to pass on your near-side. Look into the side road for obstructions such as parked cars or roadworks. Give way to pedestrians crossing the new road. Wait in this position until your way is clear.

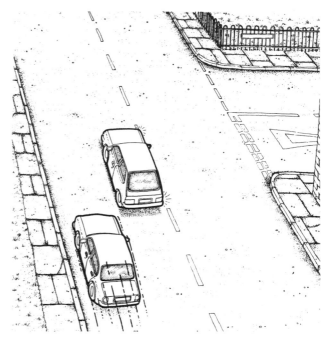

Maintain your position until the road is clear

Wait in position before turning right

Dangers to avoid when turning right

Remember when turning right the correct position for your car is just to the left of the centre of the road. Maintain this position up to the point of turn and avoid wandering back to the left.

Avoid wandering back to the left

Sometimes you will have to think about turning right from a different position.

Meet oncoming traffic safely. Watch out for vehicles approaching in the middle of the road. Keep well to the left until you can safely move into the correct position for turning.

Turning right from a different position

How to avoid cutting right-hand corners

Move up to the point of turn and make sure you can see into the new road before turning. Watch out for vehicles approaching the end of the road and avoid cutting the corner by turning into your own side of the road.

Avoid cutting corners

Pay attention when turning right where your view of oncoming traffic is limited

Cross oncoming traffic safely when turning right. Sometimes your view ahead may be restricted near bends and hill crests. There may be an approaching vehicle just out of sight. Try not to rush across.

Before you commit yourself to the turn, stay in your position just left of the centre until you can see into the new road. Go a little further forwards before turning if necessary.

Your view may be restricted

How to approach the end of a road

Approaching T-junctions

Approach the end of roads slowly enough to give yourself plenty of time to look into the main road. There are usually hedges or buildings restricting your view of traffic. If you stop too soon you won't be able to see properly.

Keep a special look-out for cyclists or motorbikes travelling along close to the kerb.

When turning right at the end of a narrow road, position the car well to the left to leave room for traffic turning in.

When you are approaching the end of a road, watch out for others who may be cutting corners. Be prepared to hold back for them.

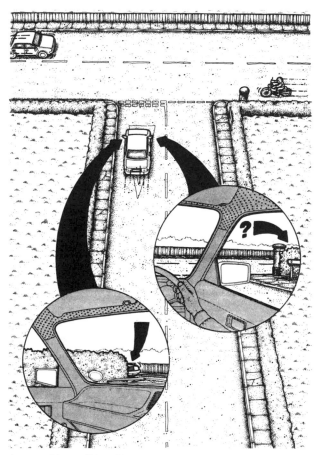

Approaching a T-junction

Be ready to give way to pedestrians

When approaching junctions, look out for pedestrians and give way to any who may be crossing the end of the road. Be particularly careful when approaching busy shopping streets.

Give way to pedestrians

Look both ways before moving into major roads

Vehicles parked near junctions will seriously restrict your view of traffic travelling along the main road.

Move slowly forwards looking both ways. Look particularly for vehicles hidden behind obstructions. Make sure you can see properly before deciding to proceed.

Watch for vehicles approaching from the left along your side of the road.

Remember: 'Creep and Peep!'

'Creep' and 'peep'

How to approach an uncontrolled crossroad

When driving along quiet side streets you will sometimes see crossroads with no signs or markings.

They are often difficult to spot. Be on the lookout for them. Watch for breaks in the hedges or building lines.

Approach slowly and be prepared to give way to traffic moving along the other road. The other driver may not have seen the danger.

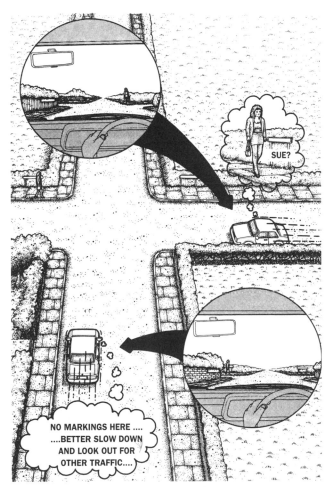

Slow down at uncontrolled crossroads

When to give way to oncoming vehicles

When vehicles are parked on your side of the road, check it is safe and move towards the centre without impeding oncoming vehicles. This position will give you a better view ahead and reduce the risk of you getting boxed in. Be ready to slow down early and hold well back to give way to oncoming traffic.

You should normally be prepared to wait in the hold-back position until you can leave a metre or so clearance.

Sometimes, to avoid traffic hold-ups, it may be necessary to proceed through much narrower spaces. To increase your safety margin, feel your way through the gap at a very low creeping speed. This will give you plenty of time to respond if anything happens, such as a driver suddenly opening a door.

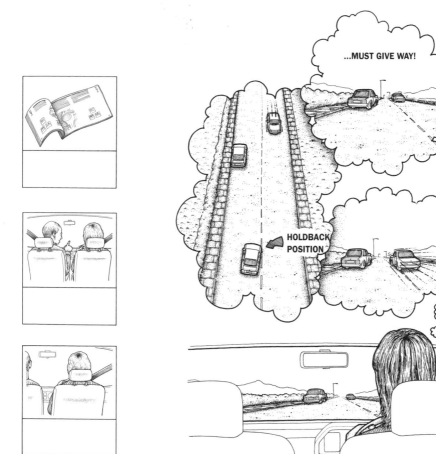

How to follow and pass cyclists safely

Stay well back from cyclists until you can give them at least 2 metres clearance without endangering oncoming drivers. Following in this position makes passing easier and prevents you from being boxed in by following drivers.

If you must overtake with less clearance, then slow right down.

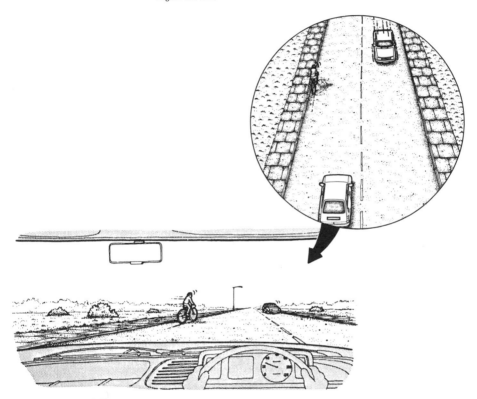

Overtake cyclists carefully

Checkpoint

1 The correct position for turning left is:
   a. half a metre from the kerb
   b. a metre from the kerb
   c. a metre and a half from the kerb
   d. 2 metres from the kerb

2 The correct position for normal driving is:
   a. as close to the kerb as possible
   b. in the centre of your side of the road
   c. half a metre from the kerb
   d. about a metre from the kerb

3 The correct hazard routine procedure is:
   a. mirror–signal–manoeuvre
   b. mirror–speed–signal
   c. signal–mirror–look
   d. speed–mirror–signal–manoeuvre

4 If pedestrians are crossing the road you are turning into you should:
   a. sound your horn loudly
   b. hold back and give way to them
   c. keep moving at the same speed
   d. wave them across so they know what you are doing

5 Where there is a stop sign at the end of a road you should:
   a. give way to all traffic in the major road
   b. only stop if you see other traffic
   c. stop at the line until safe to proceed
   d. keep moving if the road is clear

6 Approaching a left bend, position:
   a. half a metre from the kerb
   b. towards the centre of the road
   c. in the centre of your lane
   d. as close to the kerb as possible

7 In a built-up area with street lights, the speed limit is usually:
   a. 45 mph
   b. 40 mph
   c. 35 mph
   d. 30 mph

8 When you see a national speed limit sign on a single carriageway road the limit is:
   a. 40 mph
   b. 50 mph
   c. 60 mph
   d. 70 mph

9 When waiting for an opportunity to overtake a cyclist you should:
   a. keep as close to the kerb as you can
   b. stay well back but towards the centre of the road
   c. get as close as you can so that you pass as quickly as possible
   d. keep checking on the situation behind you

10 The correct sequence is:
   a. speed–position–look
   b. look–speed–position
   c. position–speed–look
   d. speed–look–position

11 The 'point of turn' is
   a. where you wait before turning right
   b. marked with white paint
   c. the line your wheels should not cross
   d. when your steering is on full lock

12 Approaching parked vehicles you should:
   a. take priority over oncoming traffic
   b. look for people crossing in between them
   c. be prepared to give way to others
   d. look for doors opening

13 You must not exceed the maximum speed limits for:
   a. the type of road you are on
   b. the type of vehicle you are driving
   c. your age group
   d. the age of your vehicle

14 If you are waiting to emerge into a main road and you cannot see because of parked vehicles you should:
   a. wait for several seconds and then go
   b. stop at the line and wait until you can see
   c. creep slowly forwards until you can see past the obstructions
   d. sound your horn so others know you are waiting

15 The main danger when turning right from a main road into a side road is:
a. following traffic
b. oncoming traffic
c. traffic ahead of you waiting to turn
d. traffic emerging from the junction

16 Clearance for parked cars should be:
a. about half a metre
b. at least a metre
c. about 2 metres
d. about a door's width

17 If there are parked cars on your side of the road you should:
a. take priority over oncoming traffic
b. give priority to oncoming traffic
c. get through as quickly as possible
d. flash your lights to encourage the oncoming drivers

18 When turning right at the end of a narrow road you should position:
a. just to the left of the white line
b. as close to the white line as you can
c. well over to the left
d. about a metre from the kerb

19 The speed limit for large goods vehicles travelling in built up areas is:
a. 20 mph
b. 25 mph
c. 30 mph
d. 35 mph

20 The speed limit for cars towing trailers on single carriageway roads outside built up areas is:
a. 35 mph
b. 40 mph
c. 45 mph
d. 50 mph

21 The speed limit for cars towing trailers on motorways is:
a. 60 mph
b. 55 mph
c. 50 mph
d. 45 mph

22 The speed limit for goods vehicles over 7.5 tonnes on motorways is:
  a. 30 mph
  b. 40 mph
  c. 50 mph
  d. 60 mph

23 As a learner you must not drive:
  a. on dual carriageways
  b. dangerously
  c. without due care and attention
  d. without reasonable consideration

24 When turning right you should position:
  a. well over to the left
  b. well over to the right
  c. just to the left of the centre of the road
  d. in any space marked for traffic turning

25 Before turning left you should not:
  a. position a metre from the kerb
  b. overtake
  c. swing out to the right
  d. pass parked cars without signalling

26 In built up areas you should look out for:
  a. road signs
  b. post boxes
  c. pedestrians
  d. vehicles emerging from junctions

27 Single track roads are only wide enough for one vehicle. You should be ready to:
  a. pull in to a passing place on the right
  b. pull into a passing place on the left
  c. wait opposite a passing place
  d. take priority over oncoming traffic

28 White reflective studs mark the:
  a. left edge of the road
  b. middle of the road
  c. lanes for traffic
  d. edge of the carriageway at lay-bys

29 You are waiting to turn right and your view ahead is
   restricted by a bend. You should:
   a. turn in as quickly as possible
   b. turn in as slowly as possible
   c. be prepared to cut the corner
   d. make sure you can see into the new road before
      turning

30 Before turning right you should ask yourself:
   a. would I be able to walk across comfortably
   b. would I be able to run across
   c. can I see clearly into the new road
   d. will I make the oncoming driver slow down

You will find the answers on page 222

Scores: 1st try ⬚ ; 2nd try ⬚ ; 3rd try ⬚ .

Record your scores in the appendix on page 225.

Manoeuvring

This stage explains how to carry out manoeuvring exercises at low speed. Start practising these as soon as you feel confident with your clutch control skills. By the time you reach Stage 8, you should be able to carry out all of these exercises with reasonable accuracy.

Only reverse where it is safe, legal and convenient. Remember, when you are manoeuvring – other road users and pedestrians have priority. You must take responsibility for checking all around so that you know you will not be inconveniencing them. Initially, your instructor will help by keeping a lookout. When practising with others in the early stages, encourage your supervisor to help with your observations.

Before practising read **The Driving Test** – pages 34–37, and learn **Highway Code** rule 71 on manoeuvring; and 176–179 on reversing.

Exercise 1 – Revise low speed control

Revise Steps 1 and 2 of Exercise 1 in Stage 4 (page 50) and practise again for a few minutes on a quiet road. Begin practising slowly driving forwards.

Exercise 2 – How to move out from behind a parked vehicle

A good test to see if you have really mastered the art of controlling the car at low speed, while working briskly on the steering, is to practise moving out from behind a parked vehicle.

Find a vehicle parked on a wide, level road and pull up about 2–3 metres (8–10 feet) behind it. You will need to control the clutch to move off much more slowly than usual. Take extra observations to the front and rear before you move off and make a final check of the blind areas before you pull out.

Consider whether you will need a signal to warn oncoming drivers as well as any approaching from behind. Use a slipping clutch as practised in Exercise 1 to keep the car creeping very slowly. Turn the wheel boldly until you are clear of the parked vehicle, then turn it back to straighten the car. Remember to look where you want the car to go.

When you have mastered the exercise on a level road practise on up and down slopes, remembering to use the footbrake to control the speed on the downhill ones.

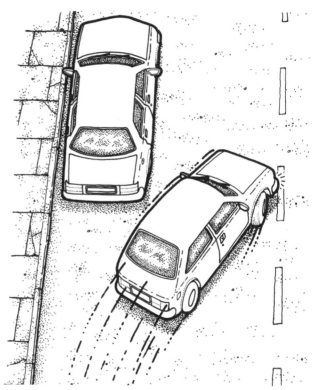

How to pull out behind a parked vehicle

Exercise 3 – How to reverse slowly in a straight line

Practise on a quiet road. Turn round in your seat until you can see the road clearly through the back window. You may remove your seatbelt for reversing if it is restricting you.

You should be able to see the kerb on both sides. Keep a special look-out for pedestrians before you start moving backwards. Look well down the road to the rear as you are reversing. Move slowly back and keep checking to the front and rear for approaching traffic.

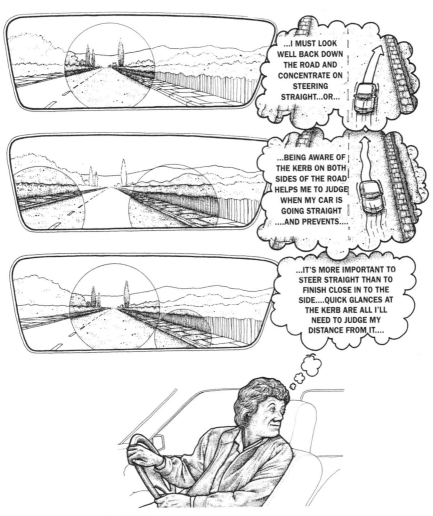

...I MUST LOOK WELL BACK DOWN THE ROAD AND CONCENTRATE ON STEERING STRAIGHT...OR...

...BEING AWARE OF THE KERB ON BOTH SIDES OF THE ROAD HELPS ME TO JUDGE WHEN MY CAR IS GOING STRAIGHT ....AND PREVENTS....

...IT'S MORE IMPORTANT TO STEER STRAIGHT THAN TO FINISH CLOSE IN TO THE SIDE....QUICK GLANCES AT THE KERB ARE ALL I'LL NEED TO JUDGE MY DISTANCE FROM IT....

How to reverse in a straight line

To make the car move towards the kerb – steer towards it.
To make it move away from the kerb – steer away from it.

If you have taken off your seatbelt remember to put it
on again before driving away.

Exercise 4 – How to drive into a parking space between two vehicles

Look and plan ahead for a suitable parking space. It will
need to be at least two and a half times the length of your
car. Remember to put the mirror–signal–manoeuvre routine
into practice. Slow down almost to a stop just before the
space, keeping about a metre (a yard) out from the parked
vehicles. Drive on slowly and steer briskly in until your front
wheel nears the kerb; then steer right to bring it into line.
Centre your car in the space by reversing if necessary.

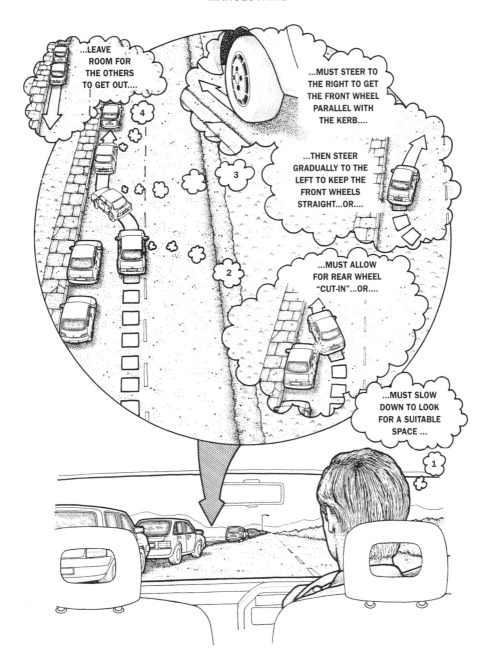

Exercise 5 – How to turn the car round in the road

This exercise is useful when there are no convenient places for reversing.

Your first attempts at this exercise should be carried out on fairly wide and level roads. Make sure there are no obstructions such as trees or streetlights on the pavement nearby.

Get the car ready for moving off in the normal manner, with the clutch slightly below the driving point. Check all around for traffic and pedestrians. When you are sure it is clear, look across the road where you intend to go and creep slowly forwards turning the wheel briskly to the right until it is on 'full lock'. When you have driven over the middle of the road, start turning the wheel back to the left. Be ready to brake if the car rolls down the camber. Keep turning the wheel to the left and stop just before you reach the kerb. Apply the handbrake.

Select reverse gear and prepare the car for moving. Check all around. When you're sure it's safe, look over your left shoulder and creep slowly back turning the wheel briskly to the left. When you have driven over the centre of the road, look over your right shoulder, turn the wheel briskly to the right. Be ready to brake if the car rolls down the camber. Keep turning the wheel to the right and stop just before reaching the kerb. Apply the handbrake.

Select first gear and get ready to move. Check all around for others. When you are sure it's safe, look well down the road and creep slowly forward turning the wheel to the right until you are in the normal driving position. Straighten the wheel, carry out the normal mirror–signal–manoeuvre routine and pull in and park on the left.

If you don't manage to complete the manoeuvre in three movements, don't worry. Simply repeat the second and third movements.

> Remember — the safety of you, your passengers and other road users is your responsibility.

Keep checking all around throughout any manoeuvre.

Turning the car around in the road

Exercise 6 – How to reverse into a road on the left

This is useful for turning round to travel in the opposite direction, for reversing into your driveway or bays in car parks.

As you drive past the road, check for any obstructions or other problems that could make your manoeuvre unsafe. Using the mirror–signal–manoeuvre routine, drive past the corner until you can see it in the interior mirror and stop about a metre from the kerb.

Turn in your seat so that you can see well down the road through the middle of the rear window. You may remove the seat belt if you feel restricted. When you have checked that it's safe all around, creep slowly back until the rear wheels are level with the corner. You can normally judge this in a car by watching the corner disappear from the rear window and reappear in the corner of the side window.

Pause at this point to have a good look around for others. If your manoeuvre is going to affect them, remember they have priority – let them make the decision to proceed or to wait for you.

When you start moving again, be aware that the front end of the car will swing out as you steer around the corner. Keep checking that it's safe and keep steering to the left until you see that the car is straight in the new road. The amount of steering you will need will depend on the sharpness of the corner. If you see someone approaching from behind, you may have to move forward to the start position to allow them to use the junction safely.

Keep looking well down the road through the middle of the rear window. This will help you judge whether the car is parallel with the kerb. To check your distance from the kerb, glance into the nearside door mirror before making your decision to stop. If you want the car to go nearer to the kerb – turn the wheel towards it. If you want to take the car away from the kerb a little, turn the wheel away from it. Any adjustments in steering at this point should be very slight.

Make sure you finish your reverse in a safe place, far enough away from the junction to allow others to use it properly. If you remove your seat belt for reversing make sure you put it on again before driving away.

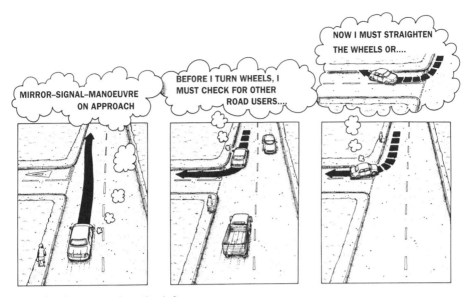

Reversing into a road on the left

Exercise 7 – How to reverse into a road on the right

This exercise is useful for turning the car round where there are no convenient places on the left, for reversing into your driveway or into bays in car parks.

Select a corner where your manoeuvre will be safe, legal and convenient. Use the mirror–signal–manoeuvre routine and take up a position as if you were going to turn right. If there are other road users around, you may have to delay your signal, otherwise they may think you are turning right.

Wait for oncoming traffic at the 'point of turn' and look into the road for any obstructions that would make your manoeuvre unsafe. Steer over to the right and stop a little out from the kerb about two car lengths past the corner. It may help to take off your seat belt and you may open your window to help you see the kerb.

Select reverse gear and prepare to move. Remember, you are manoeuvring on the wrong side of the road. You are more vulnerable, keep looking all around and respond to others. When you're sure it's clear, move slowly back looking over your left shoulder as you approach the corner. When you near the corner, pause and check all around again. Now look over your right shoulder and start steering to the right when your rear wheel is level with the corner. Steer to follow the kerb. How much steering you need will depend on how sharp the corner is.

Remember, your front end will swing out as you go round the corner. Keep checking for others and respond to what they are doing.

When you have turned the corner look over your left shoulder again. This will help you judge whether or not your car is straight in the new road. You will also be able to see what is happening behind you and to respond to others.

When your car is straight, turn the wheel to the left sufficiently to keep it straight. Remember any final adjustments should only be slight. Check your distance from the kerb by using your nearside door mirror.

To complete the exercise, drive far enough into the side road so that you have room to get back on to the left side of the road to approach the junction properly. This will also allow others to use the junction safely.

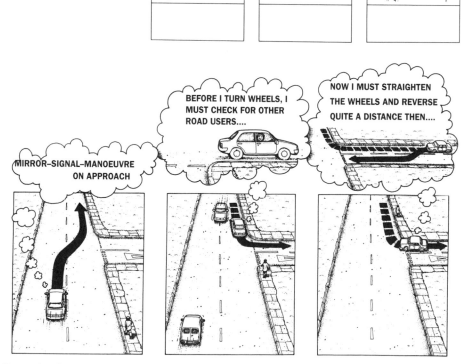

Reversing into a road on the right

Exercise 8 – How to reverse into a parking space (parallel parking)

Start practising this manoeuvre when you can carry out all of the other exercises reasonably well.

Make sure you will not be disrupting the traffic and that the place you choose is legal and safe. By the time you master the exercise you should be able to reverse into a space about one and a half times the length of your car.

Use the mirror–signal–manoeuvre routine to position your car for the exercise. You can let others know of your intentions by:

- using a left indicator or arm signal for slowing down;

- the brake lights;

- by selecting reverse gear as soon as possible.

Position yourself just beyond the front of the other vehicle and about a metre away from it. Select reverse and check all around for other road users.

When you're sure it's safe, move back slowly until the rear of your car is level with the other one. Pause, check all around and respond to others. Turn the wheel briskly to the left to steer into the space. When the rear of your car has reached the centre of the space, straighten the wheels and continue moving back, making sure your car is clearing the vehicle in front.

When the front end is clear, steer briskly to the right to straighten the car in the space. Look through the rear window and make any steering adjustments necessary to finish straight and reasonably close to the kerb. Remember you can use the nearside door mirror to check how close you are. Be polite, centre your car in the space.

Carrying out this manoeuvre slowly will allow you more time to see how the car is responding to your steering and also to give you plenty of time to make any necessary adjustments. It also means that you will be able to respond properly if there are other road users about.

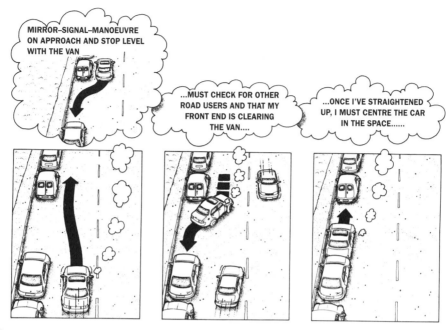

Reversing into a parking space

Checkpoint

1 Before reversing you should:
   a. sound the horn
   b. make sure the road is clear
   c. switch on the hazard flashers
   d. switch on the indicator

2 If you are unable to see when reversing you should:
   a. sound the horn
   b. get someone to help
   c. switch on your lights
   d. take a walk around the car

3 To turn the car round safely you should:
   a. reverse into a side road to drive out
   b. drive into a side road to reverse out
   c. use someone's driveway
   d. manoeuvre as quickly as possible

4 When reversing your car will respond:
   a. the same
   b. differently
   c. to other road users
   d. to road conditions

5 When turning the car round in the road you should:
   a. complete the exercise in three movements
   b. keep full control of the vehicle
   c. take priority over other road users
   d. give priority to other road users

6 Before reversing in between two cars position your car:
   a. as close as possible to the leading car
   b. reasonably close to the leading car
   c. level with or slightly ahead of it
   d. well ahead of it

7 Before reversing you should:
   a. switch on your hazard flashers
   b. ensure no danger will be caused
   c. always remove your seatbelt
   d. switch on your indicator

8 When turning round in the road you should
   a. keep the car moving slowly
   b. keep the car moving quickly
   c. turn the steering wheel slowly
   d. turn the wheel briskly

9 Before reversing you should first:
   a. turn round in your seat
   b. remove your seatbelt
   c. take off the handbrake
   d. remove the head restraint

10 When parking in between two vehicles:
   a. centre your car in the space
   b. park your car close the one in front
   c. park your car close to the one behind
   d. finish half a metre from the kerb

11 When reversing you should normally:
   a. take priority over other road users
   b. give priority to other road users
   c. ignore the other road users
   d. let the other road users decide

12 Reversing into a road on the right is useful when:
   a. the road is very wide
   b. you are in an estate car
   c. you are in a van
   d. you can't see through the rear window

13 Reversing into a space between two vehicles will require a space of:
   a. three times the length of your car
   b. two and a half times its length
   c. twice the length of your car
   d. one and a half times its length

14 Try not to reverse or turn round:
   a. in a busy road
   b. where there are lots of pedestrians
   c. on quiet estate roads
   d. where it would be lawful

15 When using a driveway you should:
   a. drive across the footpath quickly
   b. drive across the footpath slowly
   c. reverse in so that you can drive out
   d. drive in so that you can reverse out

16 You must not reverse:
   a. further than is necessary
   b. less than is necessary
   c. from a main road into a side street
   d. from a side street into a main road

17 Before reversing you should:
   a. use all of your mirrors
   b. check there are no pedestrians
   c. only look through the side windows
   d. mainly look through the rear window

18 When reversing you should:
   a. look at the kerb as a guide
   b. use a marker in the rear window
   c. look where you want the car to go
   d. mainly use the mirrors

19 When reversing round corners you should be aware that you need to steer:
   a. in the opposite direction to that which you want the car to go
   b. in the same direction as that which you want the car to go
   c. as slowly as possible for sharp corners
   d. as briskly as you would to go forward around a sharp corner

20 When reversing round corners, you should be aware that:
   a. the front end will swing out
   b. the rear end will swing out
   c. neither end will swing out
   d. only the wheels will stick out

21 When reverse parking you should not:
   a. bother about other road users
   b. cause danger to other road users
   c. park too close to the kerb
   d. take more time than is reasonable

22 When reverse parking you should not:
   a. turn the wheel while stationary
   b. carry out the exercise under slow control
   c. swing your car from side to side
   d. use effective observations

23 When positioning to reverse round a corner to the left you should:
   a. carry out the mirror–signal–manoeuvre routine
   b. be careful when timing your signal
   c. position as close to the kerb as possible
   d. position a little way from the kerb

24 When positioning to reverse round a corner on the right you should:
   a. not bother with the mirror–signal–manoeuvre routine
   b. only signal if necessary
   c. pull across to the other side of the road as early as possible
   d. wait until nearly past the end of the road before you pull across.

You will find the answers on page 223

Scores: 1st try [   ]; 2nd try [   ]; 3rd try [   ].

Record your scores in the appendix on page 225.

Gaining experience and using common sense

Introduction

Now that you are confident with your car control skills, you should prepare for your driving career by gaining experience on busier roads and in more traffic.

You will only build up your confidence by taking things one step at a time. You should first of all practise in your nearest town or outskirts of the city. Gradually work your way nearer to the town centre as your confidence increases. Get plenty of practice on as wide a variety of roads as possible. If you live in a rural area your instructor may advise you to have longer lessons to incorporate these. If you live in the town you may have to learn to deal with these situations earlier on in your course. Practise driving in laned traffic; on dual carriageways; around roundabouts; in one-way systems.

Read Parts 6, 7, and 8 of **The Driving Manual**. Learn the following **Highway Code** rules:

112–121	Lane discipline
146–166	Road junctions
167–175	Pedestrian crossings
265–272	Railway level crossings
273–278	Tramways

How to avoid accidents with other vehicles in front and behind

Follow other vehicles at a safe distance. Stay even further back from large or slow-moving ones. This improves your view of the road and of traffic ahead and helps you to anticipate the actions of the driver in front. You get more time to respond.

When other drivers are following you too closely, drop even further back from the vehicle ahead. This gives you more breathing space and extra time to brake gently which in turn gives the driver behind more time to respond.

Learn to put into practice the 'two-second rule'. When you are following a vehicle, look for an object at the side of the road such as a tree. As the vehicle ahead passes this object say to yourself: 'Only a fool breaks the two second rule'. If you are still speaking as you pass the object, you are following too closely. If you pass it after you have finished, you are keeping a safe distance. Revise **Highway Code** rule number 105.

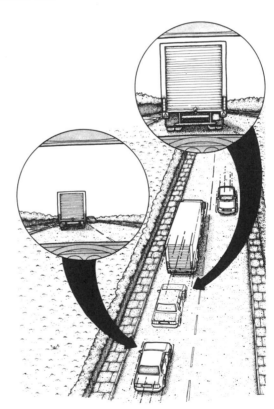

Follow at a safe distance

How to act on signals given by other road users

Watch out for signals given by the drivers of vehicles in front and anticipate their actions. When a signal is flashing, the driver is almost sure to slow down for the manoeuvre. Expect this and carry out your safety routine by checking to see what is happening behind.

If the vehicle ahead is turning right, position your car well to the left and decide whether or not there is room to pass on the nearside. Remember the other driver may have to wait for oncoming traffic. Be prepared to slow down and wait if the space is too small to get through safely.

If the driver in front is signalling left, the vehicle may be either stopping or turning. Move into an overtaking position, but hold well back as drivers waiting in the side road may emerge.

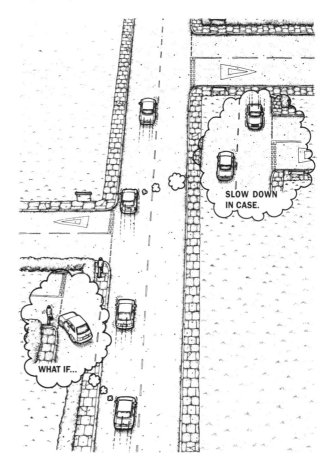

Even when you are sure the driver in front is turning, he may still have to stop and wait if the side road is blocked or if there are any pedestrians crossing. Keep well back.

Stay alert to what is happening behind

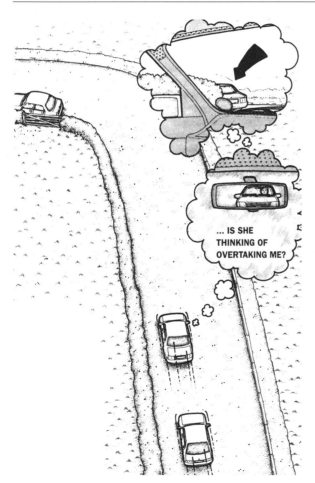

... IS SHE THINKING OF OVERTAKING ME?

On the approach to a bend, consider the action you may need to take if there is a car parked just out of sight. Check your mirror beforehand so you know in advance what is happening behind. Assess how close other vehicles are, how fast they are travelling and whether they are likely to overtake you.

When the obstruction comes into view, you already have the information to decide instantly whether you need to give a signal. You should also have decided whether it is safe to pull out, or whether you must hold back to let the following driver overtake. Checking the mirror again before pulling out should merely confirm what you already know.

Deciding if you need to signal

Signals do not give you the right to carry out your intentions regardless of others!

Use your mirrors regularly and act on what you see in them. Give signals only when you are sure that your actions will be safe. Parked vehicles can usually be seen by following drivers. If you use unnecessary signals, the driver behind may eventually ignore them. This can lead to possible danger if you wish to turn right and your signal is being ignored.

After giving a signal check around to see how others are responding to it. If you are not sure whether or not a signal is necessary it is usually advisable to use one.

Signals for passing parked vehicles may be useful when:

- a driver is following very closely or catching up quickly;

- there is already traffic in the lane to your right;

- an obstruction is just over the brow of a hill;

- there are poor light or foggy conditions.

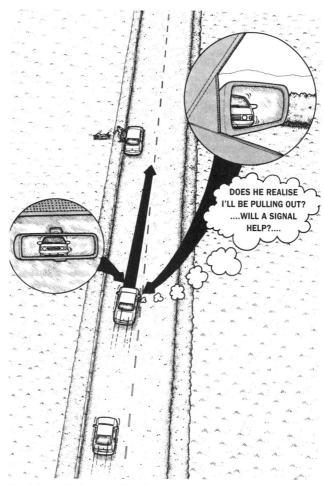

DOES HE REALISE
I'LL BE PULLING OUT?
....WILL A SIGNAL
HELP?....

Deciding whether to signal

Deciding when to signal

Signals should normally be given early so that others have time to respond. Some signals, however, need to be delayed; for example, if you want to turn left and have yet to pull out to pass a parked vehicle.

When taking a second turning on the left, wait until you are just passing the first before signalling. Drivers in the first road may pull out if they think you are turning in. However, try to give as much warning as possible to following drivers.

Signals given at the wrong time may panic others into taking unnecessary evasive action. Before giving any signal you should consider its effect on others. For example, delay a right-turn signal for changing lanes when drivers behind are overtaking you.

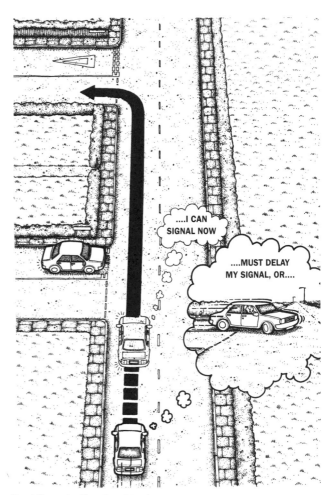

Deciding whether to signal

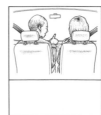

What to look out for when approaching pedestrian crossings

Look and plan well ahead. Watch out for, and give precedence to, pedestrians on zebra crossings. Look for people standing near or moving towards crossings and try to work out in advance whether they are likely to cross. Check what is happening behind and be ready to slow down. You must be travelling at such a speed that you can pull up safely if they step out.

Watch out for people near crossings

If your view of either side of the crossing is blocked by parked vehicles or other obstructions, slow down as if people were crossing. Be ready to stop until you can see it is safe to continue.

Remember, when you are parking, stop well away from any kind of pedestrian crossing!

Be ready to stop if you cannot see both sides

Approaching zebra crossings

Treat a zebra crossing with a refuge in the middle as two separate crossings. If someone steps off the pavement on to the other half you may still proceed. However, you must watch out for anyone nearing the central reserve. They may walk straight through the reserve on to the second half.

You must not overtake on the approach to pedestrian crossings. When driving in laned traffic, where there are vehicles in another lane waiting at a crossing, you may pull level with the leading vehicle but do not proceed in front of it.

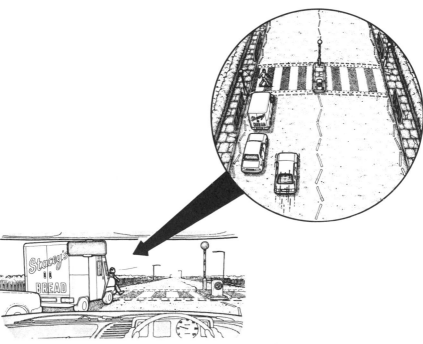

Do not overtake at pedestrian crossings

How to approach zebra crossings

Look well ahead. Where you see pedestrians waiting to cross, check your mirror and slow down. If you hold back early enough they may have time to go before you reach the crossing. Try to make eye contact with anyone waiting. This helps reassure them that they have been seen.

If you have time, give an arm signal for slowing down. This lets the pedestrians know what you are doing and also warns oncoming drivers that you are stopping.

Do not give any other kind of invitation for people to cross. Other drivers may not be stopping.

Some pedestrians find it more difficult than others to cross the road. For example, you should allow extra time for the old and infirm. Be patient with them. People with prams cannot put a foot on to the crossing to claim priority. They will have to push the pram out. Others with small children also need more time. Young people are often impulsive and may dash out on to the crossing.

If the pedestrians are walking from your right to left, wait until they are on the pavement before moving away. If they are walking from left to right, give precedence to them, but you do not need to wait until they are completely across.

However, do not startle or hurry them by driving too close or too fast. Wait until they are least three quarters of the way over.

Remember before moving away to check to the sides for other pedestrians in your blind spots.

Do not startle pedestrians

What to do at pelican crossings

Look well ahead and anticipate the lights changing. Look to see if the 'wait' sign is showing for the pedestrians. Check what is happening behind, slow down and be prepared to stop if the lights change.

If the amber light is flashing, give precedence to people who are already on the crossing. When they have crossed you may proceed.

After the lights start flashing, watch out for people making a last-minute dash. Be prepared to let them cross, but do not invite others on to the crossing.

Flashing amber does not automatically mean 'go'

How to approach traffic lights

Look and plan well ahead and anticipate lights changing. All colours except green mean stop and you should always be travelling at a speed at which you can pull up safely.

Working things out as you approach will help speed up your reactions. Check your mirrors to see how close following vehicles are and how fast they are travelling. Continually assess what you will do if the lights change.

When approaching a red light, check your mirrors and be prepared to slow down. If the light stays red, you will be able to stop comfortably. Apply the handbrake and select neutral. If the light changes to green you may continue, but remember, green means go only if it is safe. Check for vehicles from all directions and watch for oncoming drivers turning across your path.

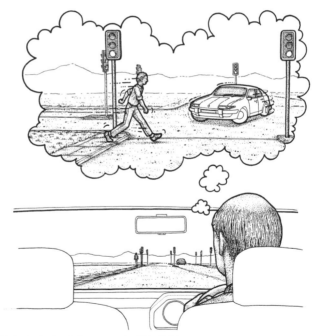

Things to look for near traffic lights

A green light can change at any time. When approaching, be aware of what is happening behind, slow down and be ready to stop if the light changes. If the green light stays on, continue but remember to check in all directions.

Look for pedestrians crossing the road you are taking and be ready to give way to them.

If your exit road is blocked, wait at the stop line – do not drive forwards and block the junction.

Where to position when turning or going straight ahead at crossroads

To drive straight ahead or turn left at a busy junction you should normally approach and stay in the left lane. Keep to this lane unless you can see reasons for selecting another.

At junctions with two or more lanes marked with arrows for going straight ahead, plan ahead and choose the most convenient one. To do this look ahead for obstructions and use your knowledge of the area.

To turn right from a busy multi-laned road, you should normally approach in the right-hand lane. One of your first priorities is to get into position early without disrupting other traffic. Check your mirrors for traffic coming up behind and to your sides and time your signal to let others know you want to move to the right. Try to maintain your speed, but be prepared to increase it so you can move safely. Reducing speed may encourage following traffic to overtake and prevent you from carrying out your manoeuvre. If this happens, hold back and wait for a larger space in the traffic. Thinking and planning well ahead should help you avoid becoming boxed in!

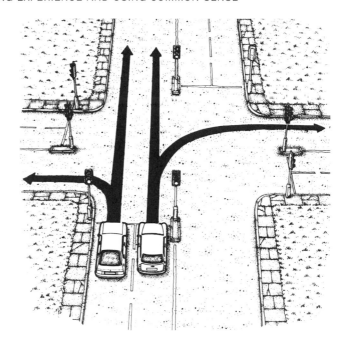

Choosing the most appropriate lane for going straight ahead

Looking and planning ahead will help you select the most appropriate lane for going straight ahead at busy junctions.

If you can see parked vehicles or other obstructions blocking the left lane at the far side of the junction, use the right-hand lane.

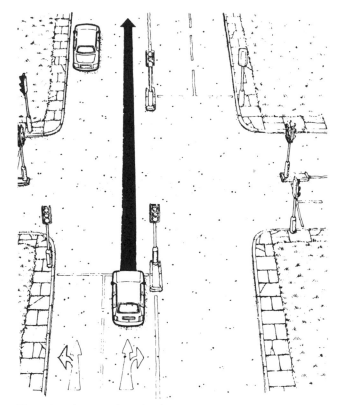

Plan ahead when choosing lanes

Choosing the most sensible lane

Watch out for right-turning vehicles ahead of you. They are sometimes held up for long periods waiting for oncoming traffic. If you position yourself behind them in the right-hand lane, you will also be delayed.

In this situation, it is normally better to choose the left lane, even where there are obstructions at the other side of the junction.

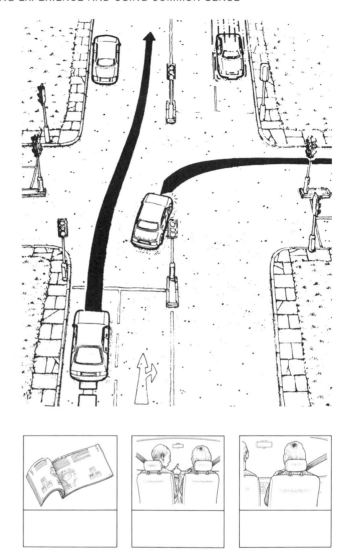

Be prepared to give way to oncoming traffic

When turning right at traffic lights, oncoming vehicles usually have a green light at the same time. Watch out particularly for traffic that is likely to travel straight through the junction or turn left. You must give way to these vehicles as it is their priority.

Wait just short of the point of turn for a suitable break in the traffic. If it is very busy, you may have to wait for the lights to change before you get an opportunity to turn. When this happens you should normally clear the junction as quickly as you can. Make sure, however, that the oncoming traffic is stopping before you proceed.

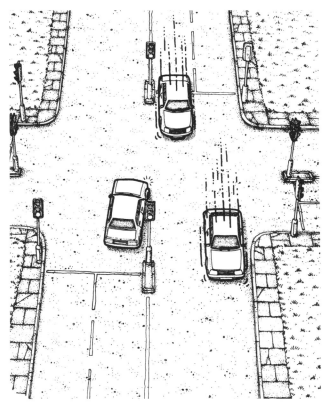

Give way to vehicles going straight ahead

What to do at filter lights

Where you see a filter arrow to the left, the nearside lane will normally be marked for left-turning traffic only. Plan well ahead and look for road markings. Avoid using this lane unless you are turning left. If you find yourself in the wrong lane, continue in that direction to avoid holding other traffic up.

When the filter arrow comes on you may turn left regardless of any other lights which may be showing. Before turning, check for other traffic moving in from your offside.

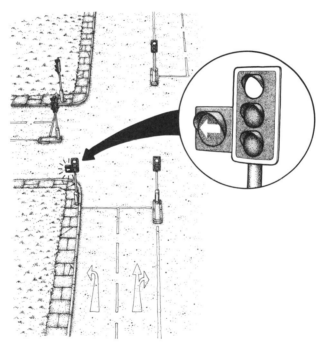

A filter arrow

Filtering to the right

Where you see a filter arrow to the right, you may turn right regardless of any other lights showing. Remember, however, that green means go if safe. Check that any oncoming traffic is stopping before you proceed.

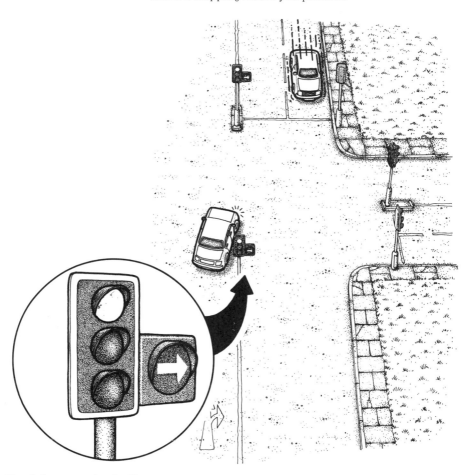

Check for oncoming traffic

How to deal with box junctions

If your exit road is not clear, wait at the stop line until you can move through the junction without blocking it.

If you are turning right and the exit road is clear, you may enter the box and wait in the centre for any oncoming traffic to pass.

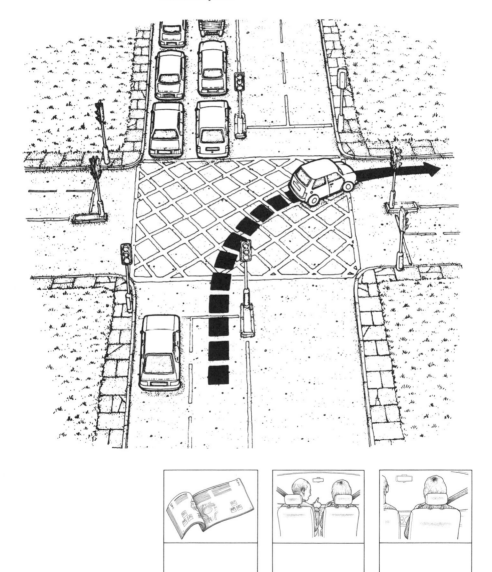

How to choose the most appropriate lane for turning left or right

Look and plan well ahead; and get into position as soon as you can. At some junctions the road markings vary from the normal rules. Where there are two or more lanes marked for the direction you wish to take, choose the most convenient one. To do this you need to know where you should be positioned at the next junction. Look, think ahead and use your knowledge of the area. At first, however, you may have to rely on your instructor for guidance.

Unless you need the right-hand lane at the next junction it is normally better to select the left lane. This will avoid you having to change lanes after the turn. If you select the right-hand lane for the turn, check carefully to the left after the turn to make sure there is no-one in your blind area before returning to the left lane.

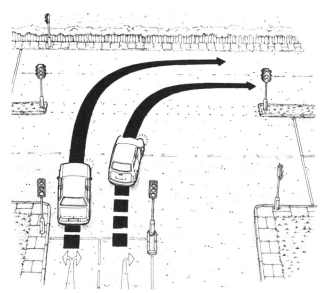

Select the most appropriate lane

Turning right at traffic lights

There are two methods of turning right at traffic lights. The method you select should depend on the:

size and layout of the junction;
road markings;
position of the oncoming vehicle;
method you feel is most appropriate if you arrive first.

How to make an offside to offside turn

This method may be appropriate at larger junctions. When the green light comes on, move slowly forward to the point of turn and steer round the rear of the oncoming vehicle. Your view ahead could be severely restricted. Give way to vehicles travelling straight through the junction. If you can't see properly – WAIT.

Unless the junction has room for more than one vehicle to wait in the junction, do not follow the leading vehicle over the stop line. You may find yourself stranded when the lights change. Wait well back until it is safe to proceed.

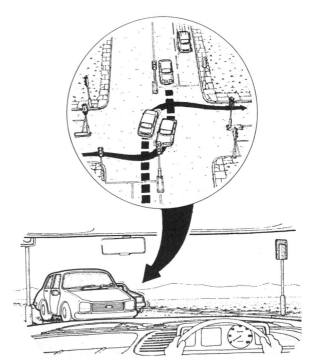

Making an offside to offside turn

125

How to make a nearside to nearside turn

This method is more appropriate at smaller junctions. It allows for more vehicles to clear the junction on a green light.

When the green light comes on, move slowly forwards steering slightly to the right. This confirms your intentions to oncoming drivers. Only turn when you are sure there is no oncoming traffic travelling through the junction. Remember to check into the new road for pedestrians or obstructions.

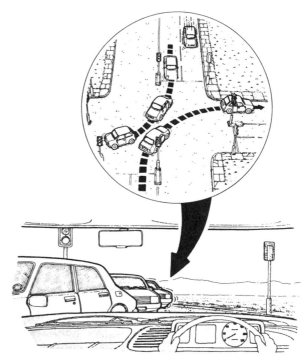

Making a nearside to nearside turn

Pedestrian crossings at traffic lights

At some busier junctions the traffic lights incorporate pedestrian crossings.

After crossing the stop line, you may have to wait for the lights changing and the oncoming traffic stopping before you can turn right. While you're waiting, look into the new road so that you know if you'll have to wait at the crossing.

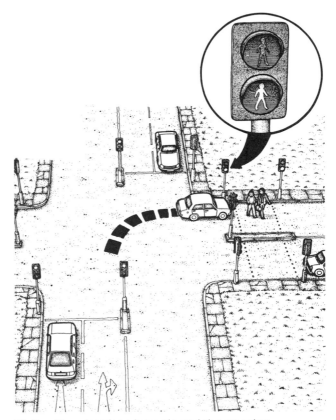

Wait until pedestrians have cleared the crossing

How to cope with driving in lanes

When driving along dual carriageways and other multi-laned roads drive in the middle of your lane. You should normally keep to the left lane unless turning right or overtaking. However, look and plan well ahead to make sure you don't get boxed in behind any parked vehicles. If you see others wanting to move out into the lane ahead of you, hold back and let them. Avoid straddling the lanes when approaching junctions and passing stationary cars or other obstructions.

Hold back to let others move out

On one-way streets take the most convenient lane for your intended direction. Expect traffic passing you on either side. Pedestrians sometimes become confused. Watch out for them stepping into the road looking in the opposite direction.

Pedestrians sometimes look the wrong way

How to make good use of the mirrors

Act sensibly on what you see in the mirrors. Simply looking in them is not enough.

Keep regular checks all around on the speed and position of other traffic – particularly on multi-laned roads. Be aware when someone has moved out of sight into your blind areas.

Drive defensively and allow others to overtake. Leave room for them to return to the lane ahead of you.

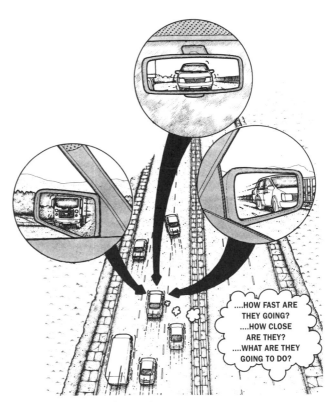

Making good use of the mirrors

Driving along dual carriageways

When driving on dual carriageways you should use your mirrors even more frequently. Look well ahead for problems and anticipate what may happen. Respond early giving those behind you time to act. Look for:

- obstructions in your lane;

- vehicles ahead slowing down;

- vehicles turning through central reserves.

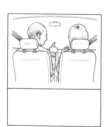

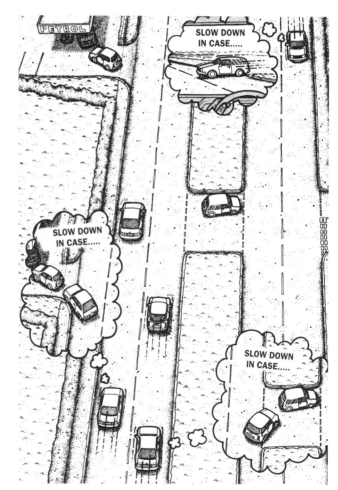

Dual carriageway driving

Turning right on to dual carriageways

When turning right on to dual carriageways, decide if there is enough room in the central reserve to offer your car protection from traffic moving along the new road. If the central reserve is wide enough to wait in, make sure you position correctly to avoid problems for drivers turning right off the dual-carriageway.

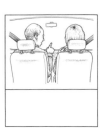

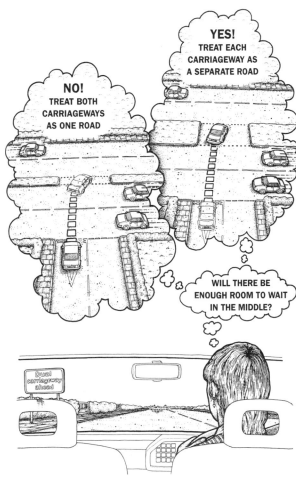

Turning on to dual carriageways

Dealing with mini roundabouts

The general rule is to 'give way to traffic from the right'. Look and plan ahead and watch for traffic already moving through the roundabout. Be ready to proceed if they're stopping the traffic on your immediate right.

You may not always have time to signal for leaving mini roundabouts – your steering is more important. Try to drive around the painted or raised area.

Dealing with mini roundabouts

How to approach roundabouts and select an appropriate position

Long before you reach a roundabout, look for the signs to, and make a mental note of, the position of your exit road. Keep checking ahead, making frequent looks to the right as you approach the junction. Try to time your arrival to coincide with a gap in the traffic. But give way to any traffic approaching from your right.

When turning left, use the mirror–signal–manoeuvre routine and approach in the left lane. Keep the signal on and stay in the left lane into the exit road.

When following the road ahead, you should normally approach in the left lane and stay in it through the roundabout. As you pass the first exit check the mirrors and give a left signal to indicate you are leaving by the next one.

When turning right, use the mirror–signal–manoeuvre routine to get into the right-hand lane. Keep the signal on and stay in the right-hand lane into and round the roundabout. As you are passing the exit prior to the one to be taken, check for vehicles in the nearside lane and make sure it is safe to cross it. Change the signal to left and leave by the next exit. You should normally leave in the left lane if it is clear.

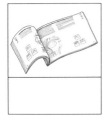

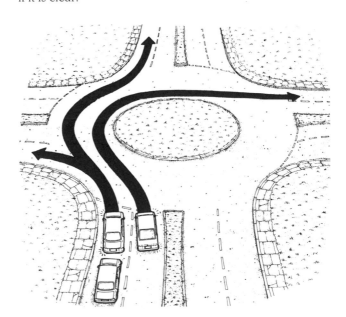

What to check when leaving a roundabout

Build up and maintain a reasonable speed on the round-about. Failing to do this, especially when you are in the right-hand lane, may result in other drivers passing on your nearside. Always check for vehicles on your left before leaving a roundabout. If the left-hand lane of the exit road is blocked or there are vehicles in the lane to your nearside, leave in the right-hand lane.

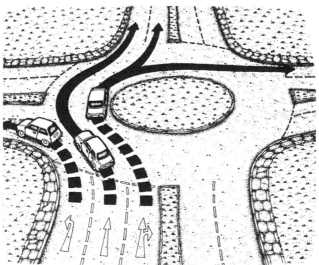

Look well ahead for road markings giving directions that vary from the basic rules. Get into position early and stay in the middle of your lane.

How to plan ahead to the next turn and choose an appropriate lane

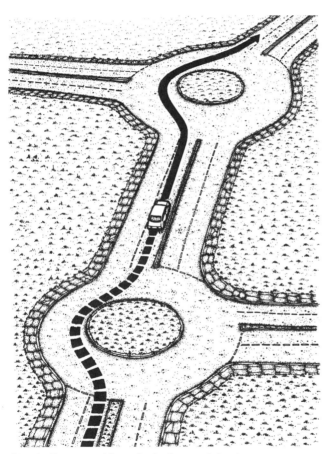

Stay in the correct lane for both roundabouts

You can avoid last-minute changes in position over short distances by working out your course in advance. To do this you need to know where you are going at the next junction and which lane you will need. Look ahead and use your knowledge of the area. At first, however, your instructor should help you with this.

When negotiating a number of junctions within a short distance of each other, choose a lane that puts you in the correct position for the next one. For example, the lane you need to approach the second of these two roundabouts will influence your position at the first. After selecting the correct lane you are able to stay in this lane throughout both turns.

 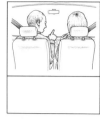 

Is overtaking necessary and is it safe?

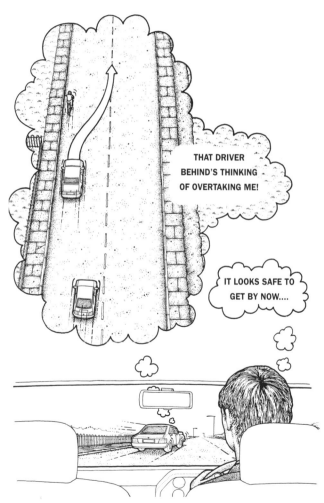

Preparing to overtake other vehicles

Before deciding to overtake, ask yourself if the benefit is worth the risk.

- Is it safe?

- Is it lawful?

- Is it necessary?

There is little point if you will be turning off shortly, if there is a line of traffic ahead and you will have to slow down, or if the vehicle ahead is driving at the speed limit.

Consider what the other driver may be doing.

- Will he or she pull out to pass a parked car or cyclist?

- Is he or she signalling to turn?

Last, but not least,

- Is it safe behind?

- Is someone overtaking you?

136

Situations in which you must not overtake

Think about the distance you will travel and also about the time you will need to overtake and get back in safely. Consider also the distance that will be covered by any oncoming vehicles.

Do not overtake where your view is restricted by bends or hill crests, or when you are approaching pedestrian crossings and side roads.

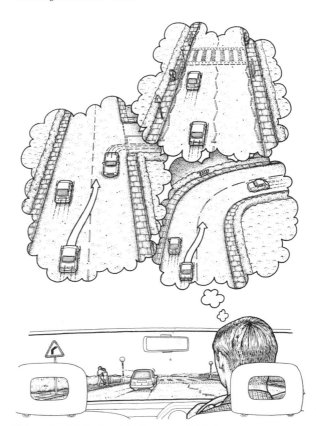

Things to think about before overtaking

Getting into position to see ahead before overtaking

The mirror–signal–manoeuvre, position–speed–look routine is slightly changed when overtaking.

To get a good view of the road ahead, stay well back and, after checking the mirror, position so that you can look along the nearside. Check the mirror again and, if safe, move over to look along the offside for a long straight stretch of road that is free of oncoming vehicles, obstructions and side turns.

Engage a lower gear, usually 3rd below 50 mph, or 2nd below 20 mph, and be ready to accelerate quickly. Look in the mirror to check that it is still safe and signal to let others know of your intentions.

Drive quickly past and, after overtaking, pull back on to your own side as soon as you can without cutting in.

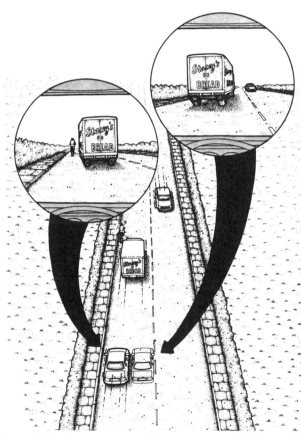

Stay well back to get a good view

Approaching level crossings

If you see a sign for a level crossing, use the mirror–signal–manoeuvre routine on the approach. A sign should tell you what kind of crossing it is. There may also be distance markers if the crossing is near a bend.

How to deal with gated level crossings

An amber light and ringing sound will be followed by a flashing red light if a train is approaching. The barriers will then come down. You must stop. The red light will continue flashing while the barrier is down. If another train is approaching the lights will continue to flash and the barriers will remain down.

If you break down on a gated level crossing, get yourself and your passengers out of the vehicle, phone the signalman and then, if there is time, push the vehicle across. Stand well clear if the bells and lights come on.

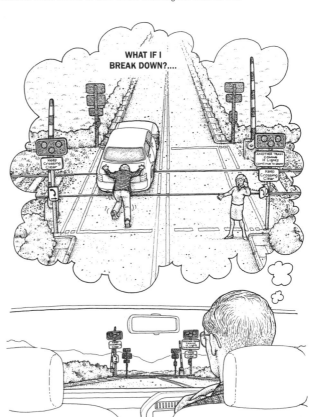

How to deal with an ungated level crossing

Some level crossings do not have gates or barriers. These will have either flashing traffic lights or 'Give Way' signs.

If for any reason you cannot clear the crossing, do not proceed on to it. A train may be approaching.

Make sure that passengers do not obstruct your view

Dealing with tramways

Treat these the same as level crossings. Look for:

tram lanes – marked by white lines;
a different type of road surface;
traffic lights;
tracks crossing the road;
the road narrowing;
pedestrians running to catch trams.

THIS TRAM'S GOING
VERY SLOWLY .... I THINK
I'LL NIP PAST .....

Overtaking trams

141

Checkpoint

1 Signals given at the wrong time can be:
   a. helpful
   b. necessary
   c. dangerous
   d. confusing

2 On a multi-laned road you should normally drive:
   a. in the centre lane
   b. in the left lane
   c. in the centre of your lane
   d. as close to the lane markings as you can

3 When following the road ahead at a roundabout with two lanes you should normally:
   a. use the left hand lane
   b. use the right hand lane
   c. use the lane with least traffic
   d. look for signs and markings

4 For leaving roundabouts you should normally:
   a. use the left hand lane
   b. use the right hand lane
   c. check over your right shoulder
   d. take the lane with least traffic

5 If you are in the wrong lane at a junction you should:
   a. follow the directions for that lane
   b. stop and wait until you can move over into another lane
   c. signal and move over quickly
   d. ask a policeman for instructions

6 When driving along in lanes in a powerful car you should:
   a. keep in the left lane
   b. keep in the right hand lane
   c. position in the centre of your lane
   d. position close to the lane markings

7 On one-way streets you should expect
   a pedestrians to be looking the other way
   b. vehicles overtaking on both sides
   c. less road signs and markings
   d. more road signs and markings

8 The flashing amber light at pelican crossings means:
a. the driver has priority
b. pedestrians have priority
c. pedestrians should now start to cross
d. you should wait for pedestrians within 50 metres of the crossing

9 At a box junction with traffic lights you should normally wait to turn right:
a. in the box for oncoming traffic
b. at the stop line for oncoming traffic
c. in the box only if your exit road is blocked
d. until the lights have changed to red

10 Following the road ahead at traffic lights your exit road is blocked, you should:
a move into the junction to wait
b. wait at the line until the exit is clear
c. move forwards and wait behind the queue
d. change lanes quickly to avoid waiting

11 When turning right at traffic lights you should:
a. give way to oncoming traffic
b. wait at the line for a break in the traffic
c. proceed because you have a green light
d. proceed on green only if it is safe

12 A green filter arrow means:
a. you may proceed only when the main green light shows
b. you may proceed if safe, regardless of the other lights
c. all the other lights will be red
d. it is safe for you to proceed

13 The first thing to do if you break down on a railway level crossing is:
a. get all passengers out of the car
b. try to push the car over the crossing
c. telephone the signalman
d. try to find out what the problem is

14 When a single carriageway road has four lanes, you should use:
a any lane for turning left
b. any lane for driving ahead
c. only the lanes that signs or markings indicate
d. the lanes which have least traffic in

15 You should give precedence to:
a   pedestrians anywhere in the road
b. only pedestrians using crossings
c. any pedestrians waiting to use pelican crossings
d. on zebra crossings

16 You should treat a zebra crossing with a central refuge as:
a. one crossing
b. two crossings
c. the same as a single crossing
d. the same as a pelican crossing

17 Dual carriageways are more dangerous than motorways because:
a. the traffic travels at higher speeds
b. traffic may turn right from them
c. traffic may turn left from them
d. traffic can overtake on either side

18 At level crossings, the flashing red light means:
a. stop and wait
b. another train may be coming
c. you have 15 seconds to cross
d. the gates will fall in 15 seconds

19 When turning right on to a dual carriageway you should:
a. work out if the central reserve is wide enough to wait in
b. check the road to the right is clear and move to the centre regardless of the width of the central reserve
c. wait until it is safe to cross both carriageways before you move regardless of the central reserve
d. make sure no-one is turning through the central reserve

20 A safe following distance at 40 mph is:
a. 20 metres
b. 2 seconds
c. 30 metres
d. 40 metres

21 If another driver is following you too closely, you should:
a. drop back from the car in front
b. flash your brake lights
c. speed up to get further ahead
d. brake earlier and more gently

22 The road used by trams is often marked with:
   a. white dots
   b. white lines
   c. yellow dots
   d. yellow lines

23 The shape of signs for tram drivers is:
   a. circular
   b. diamond
   c. square
   d. triangular

24 In areas where there are trams you should:
   a. sometimes give way to trams
   b. always give way to trams
   c. try to get away to race trams
   d. not try to race or overtake trams

25 Open railway level crossings have:
   a. no gates
   b. lower barriers
   c. Give Way signs
   d. attendants

26 Toucan crossings are shared by:
   a. car drivers and pedestrians
   b. pedestrians and cyclists
   c. cyclists and motorcyclists
   d. motorcyclists and pedestrians

27 Puffin crossings are designed to:
   a. enable people with animals to cross in safety
   b. improve road safety
   c. reduce unnecessary delays to traffic
   d. stop traffic for longer to allow people with disabilities
      to cross

28 In the light sequence at puffin crossings there is:
   a. a steady amber light
   b. no steady amber light
   c. a flashing amber light
   d. no flashing amber light

29 At puffin crossings an electronic device:
   a. detects when cars are approaching
   b. detects when pedestrians are on the crossing
   c. speeds up the green light for drivers
   d. delays the green light for pedestrians

30 The zigzag lines at all pedestrian crossings mean you must not:
a. stop
b. park
c. overtake
d. drive over them

You will find the answers on page 223

Scores: 1st try ⬚; 2nd try ⬚; 3rd try ⬚

Record your scores in the appendix on page 225.

Learning to anticipate problems and avoid accidents

Introduction

One life lost in an accident is one life too many. Road accidents cost far too many lives, leave a great number of people seriously injured and cost millions of pounds every year.

It has been shown that, by learning to how to anticipate and avoid problems, accidents can be reduced by as much as 50 per cent.

Your car control skills should now be well developed and you should have dealt with most types of hazards. You should also have learnt from experience that other drivers don't always do what they should do.

This section shows you how to anticipate what might happen and explains how you can avoid accidents by driving defensively.

Read Part Ten of **The Driving Manual** and learn the following **Highway Code** rules:

90–91	Flashing headlights
92	Horn
103–104	Speed limits
105	Stopping distances
125	Consideration
126	Concentration
127–128	Mobile phones and in-car technology
132	Country roads
133	Single track roads
180–193	Road users requiring extra care
194	Emergency vehicles
195–197	Powered vehicles and large vehicles
198–199	Buses, coaches, trams and electric vehicles
200	Vehicles with flashing amber lights
201–212	Adverse weather conditions
213–226	Waiting and parking

You must concentrate all the time

So that you pay full attention to what's happening all around you, you must:

- concentrate;

- read the road well ahead;

- know what's going on all around you, and;

- be ready to respond in good time to avoid problems.

If you're not feeling at all well, you should consider delaying your journey. You'd be surprised how even a common cold can affect your concentration.

Try to delay your journey if unwell

Be sensible with your speed

Remember – a speed limit is not a target. It is the highest permitted speed for that area. This means it will not always be safe to travel up to that speed.

The speed at which you drive should depend on the road, the weather, and traffic conditions.

> When you double your speed – braking distance increases by four times. Always travel at a speed at which you can stop *safely*!

Watch your speed

Accidents cost lives

Be prepared to give way, even if it may be your priority. No matter who causes an accident, the result is the same:

INJURY DAMAGE EXPENSE INCONVENIENCE MISERY!

The consequence of accidents

Experience will teach you that other drivers make mistakes.

When you see a possible problem, check your mirrors, adjust your speed and give yourself time to react. Continually look and plan ahead. Near junctions, expect others to move into or across your path.

In areas where your view may be restricted, for example near parked vehicles, expect pedestrians to be walking, or even running, into the road.

Watch for other road users' mistakes

Be patient

In today's volume of traffic you must expect delays in your journeys. You should allow plenty of time, especially if you are driving in peak traffic hours.

Even though you have been taught to drive confidently there are many others on the road less able than yourself. Be ready to wait patiently. If there are very few gaps in the traffic it's a waste of time losing your patience – there's nothing to be done about it. If you get annoyed it will affect your own safety and you will be tempted to take risks.

If you are driving properly and keeping to the speed limits don't let drivers behind push you. Keep calm and, if they get too close, drop a little further back from the vehicle ahead of you to increase your braking distance. If you feel threatened, it may even be sensible, when it is safe, to pull in to the left and let them get by.

Display tolerance towards other drivers

Most accidents result from the fault of one, or more drivers and others not taking action and driving defensively.

The next picture shows one of the most common accident-prone situations. The first driver has parked thoughtlessly opposite the junction. The second driver is passing the parked car without considering what may happen if a vehicle comes out from the junction. The driver emerging from the junction is not looking properly to the left nor considering the possibility of anything approaching from that direction.

As a safe driver you should:

- park where it is safe;

- consider vehicles emerging from junctions – even when it is your priority;

- look carefully in all directions before emerging from junctions.

Silly mistakes can lead to accidents

Concentrate on your driving!

Traffic situations can change very quickly. If you have passengers, keep your eyes on the road when you talk to them.

The use of any in-car entertainment systems or telephones can also be a distraction. Radios can be useful for traffic reports and light background music. Serious listening to plays or other heavy programmes, however, can affect your concentration.

Telephones, unless hands-free, should not be used while you are on the move. Find somewhere safe to stop to answer or make calls. Remember, any telephone conversation can be a distraction – even when using a hands-free model.

Changing tapes and CDs means looking away from the road and taking a hand from the wheel. Try to avoid this especially when driving at higher speeds, in heavy traffic, and around corners and roundabouts.

Smoking can be dangerous to your health – especially if you do it while driving and you drop your cigarette.

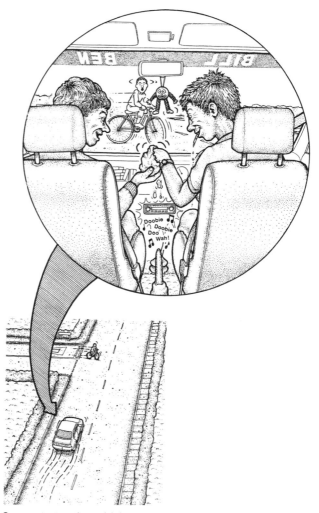

Concentrate when driving

Dealing with oncoming vehicles

Always be prepared to give way to oncoming drivers, even though it may be your priority. Look well ahead and when you see a vehicle parked on the other side of the road, expect oncoming drivers to keep coming. Check what is happening behind and ease off the gas. This will give you time to work out whether the other driver is going to make you wait or whether you can keep moving.

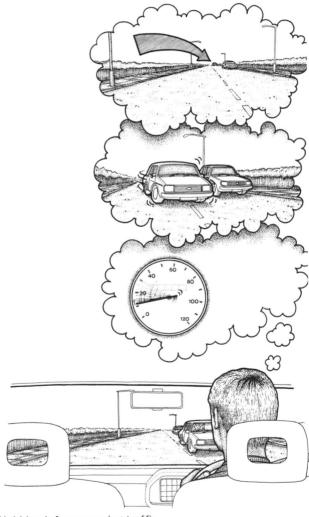

Hold back for oncoming traffic

Watch out for oncoming drivers turning right

You shouldn't always expect drivers turning right to wait for you.

When you see a vehicle approaching with a right signal on, try to work out its speed. If it does not appear to be slowing down enough, check to see what is happening behind and ease off the gas. Hold back if you think it will turn in front of you.

If you're driving ahead at traffic lights, watch for drivers turning across your path. They may not have seen you.

Watch out for right turning drivers

Watch out for drivers emerging from side roads

Even when you're driving along major roads, you should expect drivers to emerge from side roads. As you're driving along, check your mirrors regularly and look ahead for roads to the left and right.

Watch for drivers approaching the junctions at high speed. They may not look properly and pull out in front of you simply because they didn't see you. Others may be hesitant and sit thinking 'Shall I go or shall I wait'. They appear to be waiting but, at the last moment, they pull out in front of you.

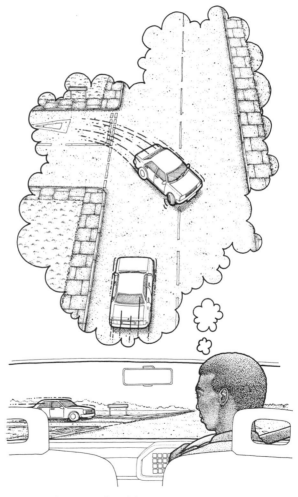

Watch out for emerging drivers

Being courteous and using eye contact

When you are waiting in traffic make sure you leave side roads and other main entrances clear for others to drive in and out.

If you are waiting to emerge from a side road, try using eye contact and smiling. This often encourages others to let you in.

Using eye contact

Changing lanes in heavy traffic

Look and plan well ahead, reading the signs and markings. This will help you get into the correct lane in good time. If you do find yourself in the wrong lane in heavy traffic, avoid trying to change lanes quickly.

Use a signal and try to make eye contact with a driver already in the lane you wish to take. When you are sure the other driver is letting you in, move over gradually and acknowledge the courtesy. Before you move, however, check in your door mirrors for cyclists and motorcyclists driving between the lanes.

How to change lanes in traffic jams

Avoiding accidents with vehicles to your sides

Make sure other drivers are aware of your presence. Avoid driving in the blind areas to their sides.

Look well ahead for obstructions and anticipate when vehicles ahead will need to change lanes. Check your mirrors regularly and be ready to let people into the lane ahead of you.

Larger vehicles often take unusual courses through bends and roundabouts. Anticipate this, keep out of their blind areas and hold back for them where necessary.

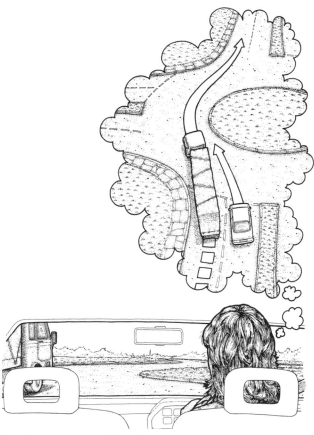

Avoiding accidents with vehicles to your sides

Allow room for larger vehicles

Their size makes it difficult for larger vehicles to negotiate some turns. They often need to swing out to the right before turning left, or position well over to the left before turning into narrow roads or entrances on the right. When you see large vehicles signalling to turn, keep well back and allow them plenty of space and time.

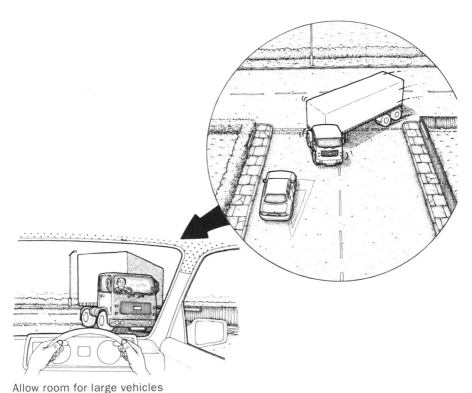

Allow room for large vehicles

Dealing with buses

Buses stop frequently, often with little warning. Stay well back from them and watch for:

- last minute signals for stopping;

- passengers standing on the bus ready to get off;

- people waiting at bus stops ahead.

When you think a bus will be stopping:

- check your mirrors;

- keep well back; and

- position to the offside in case you can get by when it stops.

When passing buses be aware that passengers may be walking into the road in front of it. Watch for feet! When coming up behind stationary buses, watch for moving out signals. Be prepared to give way where it is safe, particularly in towns.

Avoiding accidents near buses and stationary vehicles

Watch out for last minute signals

Avoiding accidents before turning

Always be aware of what is behind you, particularly before you decide to turn.

Follow the mirror–signal–manoeuvre routine and take a final look in the appropriate door mirror before turning right or left. Remember, if you use your mirrors properly and react to what you see in them, you should not have the problem shown in the illustration.

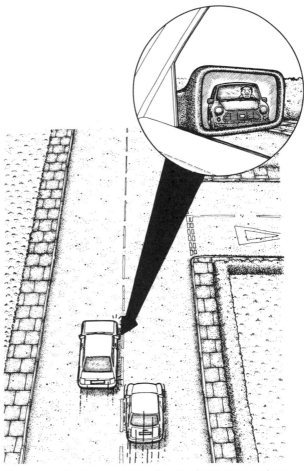

Make sure that passengers do not obstruct your view

Dealing with emergency vehicles

Pay attention at all times and stay alert. If you listen to any in-car entertainment don't have it so loud that it could mask outside noises such as sirens. Use your mirrors regularly and look and listen. If you hear an emergency vehicle approaching consider its route. Be ready to take any necessary safe action to let it pass.

Remember – someone's life may be at stake.

Dealing with emergency vehicles

Anticipating problems before you see them

There could be anything around a bend or over a hill. Wherever you can't see the road ahead, anticipate that there will be some sort of problem and then you will be ready for it when it appears. Check your mirrors and be prepared to slow down so that you will be able to stop within the distance you can see is clear.

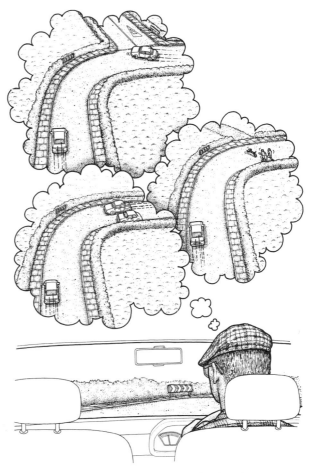

Things to think about when approaching bends

Anticipating problems in busy areas

Areas where there are lots of parked vehicles hide all sorts of problems from the driver. Remember you may have to drive well below the speed limit in built-up areas. You need to:

- look through car windows for signs of movement;

- leave plenty of clearance, allowing for doors opening;

- look out for hidden junctions – others may be emerging;

- watch for pedestrians walking between parked cars;

- allow for the erratic actions of cyclists.

Be prepared to wait for oncoming vehicles. You may have to pull into or opposite a space to allow them room to get through.

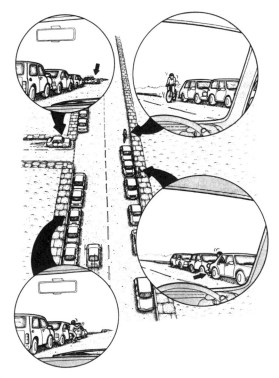

What to look out for near parked vehicles

Anticipating the actions of pedestrians

A high proportion of pedestrians killed in road accidents are either under 15 or over 60. They often misjudge the speed and distance of traffic and may step unexpectedly into the road.

Be patient with the old and people with disabilities. Give them plenty of time and don't harass them. Watch out at all times for pedestrians in or near the road, particularly when driving:

- in shopping areas;

- near schools;

- near junctions;

- around ice cream vans and other mobile shops;

- near bus stops.

Look well ahead and be prepared to slow down, leaving plenty of clearance in case anyone steps into the road. Sometimes a light tap on the horn can draw attention to your presence. Be particularly careful near schools, not all of the older children feel the need to cross safely with the crossing patrol.

Be prepared to move out to avoid pedestrians

Avoiding accidents with pedestrians

All pedestrians have priority!

When you are turning into entrances or drives, give way to pedestrians on the pavement. It's far safer to drive forwards out of drives and entrances, so, wherever you can do so, reverse in. If you're driving out where your view is restricted, be prepared to sound your horn. If you do have to reverse out, more care will be needed. Move back slowly checking all around for pedestrians throughout your manoeuvre. Be prepared to stop and wait.

Children tend to be impulsive, particularly when they've just come out of school. Check the mirrors, slow down and be ready to stop.

Reverse slowly and look before moving back

Avoiding accidents near bends

Sometimes pedestrians walk in the road, for example in country lanes or when the pavements are slippery.

Watch out for joggers, particularly at night. They can be difficult to see. Wherever you are, you should expect hazards. When you are approaching bends and hill crests, especially where there are no pavements, expect to meet people walking in the road. Check your mirrors and be ready to slow down or stop.

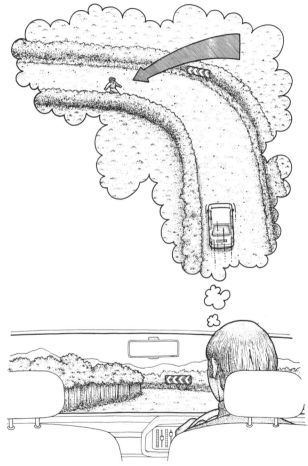

Things to think about when approaching bends

Avoiding accidents with cyclists

The closer you get to them the more cyclists will wobble. Allow plenty of room for this. If you can't give at least 2 metres clearance, then slow right down so that you can stop safely if they cycle into your path for any reason.

When emerging from junctions, watch for cyclists and motorcyclists riding close to the kerb. Make sure you look properly whatever the conditions, but particularly in poor light and bad weather. **Be patient and expect the unexpected.**

Anticipate the actions of cyclists – part 1

Cyclists don't always check behind before they pull out to pass obstructions. Check your mirrors, slow down and expect them to steer out at the last moment.

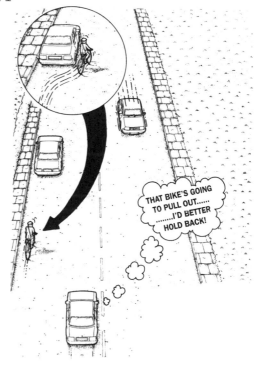

Anticipate the actions of cyclists – part 2

Using the mirrors to avoid accidents with cyclists and motorcyclists

Before you turn left or move away at a pedestrian crossing, check your nearside door mirrors. When driving in lanes check all mirrors for cyclists and motorcyclists driving in between them.

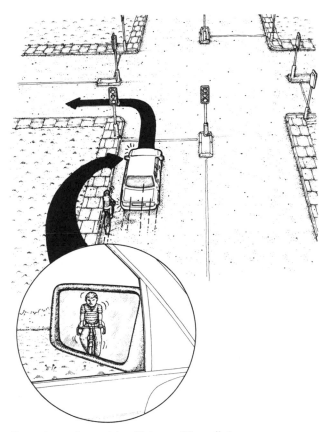

Use mirrors to avoid collisions with cyclists

Avoiding accidents with animals

Always expect the unexpected! If you see a dog off a lead, it could run across the road. It may then run back again! Check your mirrors and be prepared to slow down or even stop.

Horses need extra care. Make sure you have enough room before deciding to pass them. Check your mirrors, slow down and select the appropriate gear before you reach them. Drive quietly past leaving as much room as possible.

Take care when approaching animals

Avoiding accidents on country roads

Concentrate and plan well ahead. Remember speed limits are the maximum allowed for the road – not targets! If you are driving on country roads drive at a speed at which you can stop within the distance you can see is clear.

Don't think that, because you're out of the hustle and bustle of town, you won't come across any hazards. The countryside holds different dangers. You never know what there may be around the next bend. Drive more slowly on narrow roads, through villages and near farm entrances.

Be prepared to give way. On single-track roads there are sometimes pulling in places. Plan well ahead and work out whether you will need to pull into one on your side, or opposite one.

Be patient when following slow-moving vehicles. Do not overtake until you are absolutely sure that it will be safe. In rural areas, expect mud in the road in wet weather.

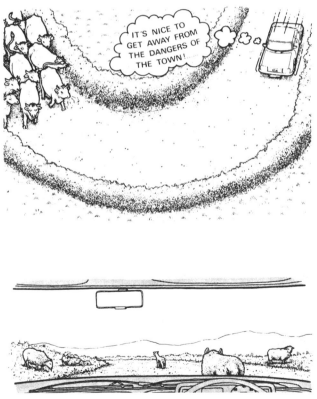

The countryside holds extra dangers

Make sure you can be seen

Lights should be used, not only when it's too dark or foggy for you to see properly, but to help others see you.

When daylight conditions are poor, or in heavy rain and snow use your dipped headlights. When visibility falls to below 100 metres use your fog lights. These should not, however, be used at other times. When used at the wrong time, high intensity rear lights can mask the brake lights so

Use dipped headlights in poor conditions

that following drivers have little or no warning that you may be slowing down. Front fog lights can dazzle and annoy oncoming drivers – use them properly.

Avoiding accidents at night

It's much harder to see at night. Your view may be masked by shadows, particularly at dusk. Watch out for pedestrians wearing dark clothing and cyclists riding without lights.

Use dipped headlights in built-up areas so that you can see and be seen.

Use full headlights where the street lighting is poor. Be ready to dip them for oncoming drivers and when you are following other vehicles so that they don't cause dazzle in the mirrors.

Dip your headlights to avoid dazzling oncoming traffic

Avoiding accidents in the fog

Only drive in foggy conditions if your journey is absolutely necessary. If you must drive, use dipped headlights. If visibility is really bad switch on the fog and high intensity rear lights. To keep down condensation in your car, use the demister and rear screen heater. A slightly open window will not only help this but, it will also help you hear other traffic before you can see it.

Don't be tempted to follow others too closely – remember they may brake suddenly. Keep your distance. Drive at a speed at which you can stop safely and remember that not all other drivers will be using their headlights.

Watch out for obstructions in the road and drive at a distance at which you can stop safely. Signals for passing parked vehicles and other hazards will become more

Drive slower in fog

necessary as it is more difficult for following drivers to see obstructions.

When waiting to turn right into minor roads, it may help to keep your foot on the brake pedal – this will give you an extra set of lights to the rear.

Driving in windy conditions

When overtaking high-sided vehicles expect to feel the wind throwing you off course as you pass by. This will be even worse in high exposed places, such as bridges. Hold the steering wheel firmly to compensate.

When driving in lanes anticipate other road users being affected.

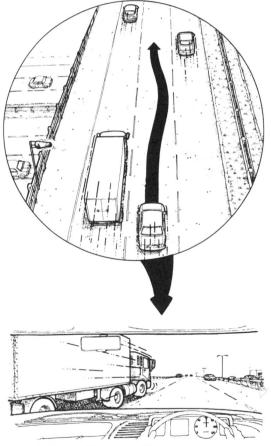

Strong winds can blow you off course

Avoiding problems by reading the road ahead

Always read the road well ahead and take the weather conditions into consideration.

Drive more slowly on wet, icy or greasy roads

Check your mirrors and slow down when you can see the road surface deteriorating. Keep off soft verges and look out for mud, gravel or chippings. When it rains after a long spell of dry weather, a combination of oil, dust, rubber and water can make the surface very slippery.

In the autumn watch for damp patches under trees where leaves can also make the surface slippery. In the winter these areas will hold frost longer than the parts of the road the sun has reached.

In freezing conditions, avoid accelerating or braking on exposed parts of the road such as bridges. There could be black ice which is almost impossible to detect.

Avoiding skids

There is only one real cause of a skid – **the driver**.

A car will only do what a driver tells it to. If you don't adapt your driving to suit the conditions you could have problems. You should:

- look and plan ahead;

- take into account the road and weather conditions;

- adjust your speed to suit the traffic conditions;

- use all of the controls gently and progressively;

- anticipate what could happen in any situation;

- travel at a speed at which you can stop safely;

- maintain a safe following distance from the vehicle ahead;

- adjust your speed if someone is following you too closely.

In snow or icy conditions you should:

- slow down early using light pressure on the brake pedal;

- accelerate gently and stay in the highest gear possible;

- when driving uphill try to keep moving steadily by keeping well back from the vehicle ahead.

Avoid unnecessary journeys in bad weather

Driving through floods and fords

Look well ahead for signs and always be aware of what is happening behind. At some fords there are gauges to tell you how deep the water may be. Slow down and change into 1st or 2nd gear and, using a slipping clutch, keep the engine revs up. Look for any camber in the road and drive slowly through at the shallowest point.

When you reach the other side you need to make sure the brakes are dry. Drive very slowly and press the brake gently with your left foot.

Avoiding aquaplaning

Aquaplaning can happen when a cushion of water is built up in front of fast moving tyres. If the tyres cannot displace the water they may ride up on to it, losing contact with the road surface. The steering will become light and you could also lose your braking control.

To avoid aquaplaning:

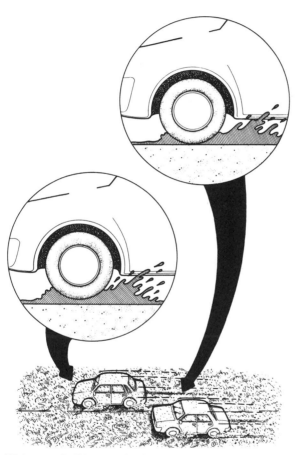

- keep your tyres in good condition and properly inflated;

- make sure your brakes are well maintained;

- plan well ahead adapting your speed to suit the conditions;

- take into account the road and weather conditions.

Water can build up under fast moving tyres

Correcting skids

The most common types of skid are caused by harsh braking or sudden steering movements at excessive speeds for the conditions.

Braking too hard can cause the wheels to 'lock up'. If this happens the car will slide along the road and braking control will be lost. The most effective way of regaining control is to remove the cause by releasing the brake and then reapplying it in an on-off/on-off pumping action.

Steering too fast into bends, especially in wet conditions, can result in the rear of the car sliding away from the centre of the corner. This 'rear wheel skid' is the most common. You will see the front end of the car being pulled away from its course and your natural reaction should be to straighten it up again. Try not to over-react. If the rear of the car swings to the right – steer to the right; if it swings to the left – steer to the left.

Your instructor may be able to advise you on skid control training as part of the Pass Plus scheme when you have passed your practical driving test.

Using steering and the brake to correct a skid

Checkpoint

1 If you must drive in fog:
   a. try to follow closely the rear lights of the vehicle in front
   b. use dipped headlights
   c. use full beam headlights
   d. keep your footbrake on when waiting to turn right off a main road

2 If you must drive in fog:
   a. allow less time for your journey
   b. allow more time for your journey
   c. make more use of your hazard warning lights
   d. drive nearer to the centre line

3 If another driver flashes the headlights it means:
   a. it will be safe for you to proceed
   b. the other driver is giving way
   c. it's a warning of their presence
   d. it is their priority

4 When driving near animals you should be ready to:
   a. slow down or stop
   b. sound your horn
   c. drive quickly away
   d. give lots of clearance

5 If you park on the road at night you use your sidelights if leaving your car:
   a. on a road with a speed limit of less than 30 mph
   b. on a road with a speed limit of more than 30 mph
   c. within 10 metres of a junction
   d. if the road is poorly lit

6 You should only flash your headlights:
   a. when you want another driver to give way to you
   b. when you are giving way
   c. to let others know you are there
   d. to encourage pedestrians to use zebra crossings

7 You should be careful and considerate to other road users. You should:
   a. expect others to take the correct action
   b. expect others to make mistakes
   c. always be ready to give way
   d. only give priority when you have no choice

8 Staying well back from a slow-moving vehicle will:
   a. give you a better view ahead
   b. help you to anticipate its actions
   c. make it easier to overtake
   d. make it more difficult to overtake

9 You should give way to buses and coaches:
   a. waiting to emerge from bus depots
   b. waiting to pull out from bus stops
   c. whenever you see them
   d. whenever you can do so safely

10 Approaching blind bends you should expect:
   a. pedestrians walking in the road
   b. other road users to be driving correctly
   c. oncoming vehicles keeping well over on their side of the road
   d. obstructions around the bend

11 The road surface can be very slippery:
   a. in the summer during a fine spell
   b. in the summer after a shower following a fine spell
   c. in any damp patches under trees
   d. if your tyres are not correctly inflated

12 Wind or side draught can affect your car:
   a. in high exposed places
   b. if you drive at high speed with your sunroof open
   c. mainly in built-up areas
   d. after overtaking a large vehicle

13 Driving errors may be caused by:
   a. concentrating too much
   b. not concentrating enough
   c. driving an unroadworthy vehicle
   d. driving when unwell

14 If a following driver becomes impatient when you are waiting to emerge into a busy road, you should:
   a. pull out as quickly as you can
   b. keep calm and wait for a safe gap in the traffic
   c. take as long as you can to teach the other driver some manners
   d. put on your high intensity rear lights to distract him

15 When driving on dual carriageways you should:
   a. rely solely on your interior mirror
   b. use all of the mirrors regularly
   c. check the blind spots before stopping
   d. look and plan well ahead

16 Driving on a fairly narrow road, you see ahead a large vehicle emerging from a road on the right. You should:
   a. expect the large vehicle to swing out into the road
   b. ignore the situation because the other driver should give way
   c. check your mirrors and steer well in to the left
   d. hold back and give the other driver plenty of room

17 The most vulnerable road users are:
   a. learner drivers
   b. pedestrians
   c. motorcyclists
   d. horse riders

18 You should drive carefully and slowly:
   a. in residential areas
   b. on straight country roads
   c. when turning at busy junctions
   d. when pavements are closed

19 Children and elderly pedestrians are particularly vulnerable, they:
   a. should be able to judge your speed
   b. may not be able to judge your speed
   c. could step out into the road
   d. should be encouraged to hurry across the road

20 If you see someone with a white cane that has two red reflective bands they are:
   a. deaf and blind
   b. deaf and mute
   c. blind and mute
   d. fitted with a hearing aid

21 If a pedestrian is hit by a car travelling at 20 mph the chance of them being killed is:
   a. 1 in 10
   b. 1 in 20
   c. 1 in 30
   d. 1 in 40

22 You should only use a hand-held mobile phone when:
   a. driving on motorways
   b. driving in towns
   c. you are stationary
   d. you want to answer a call

23 On country roads you should expect:
   a. partially hidden junctions and entrances
   b. pedestrians walking in the road
   c. farm animals to be kept under control
   d. farmers to clear mud from the road

24 You should look and listen for emergency vehicles. The flashing lights they may be using are:
   a. amber
   b. red
   c. green
   d. blue

25 Emergency vehicles may also use:
   a. headlights
   b. hazard warning lights
   c. sirens
   d. radio controlled loudspeakers

26 When an emergency vehicle approaches you should:
   a. try not to panic
   b. consider its route
   c. speed up to get out of the way
   d. take safe action to let it pass

27 At night when visibility is more than 100 metres you should use:
   a. dipped headlights
   b. sidelights and spot lamps
   c. sidelights and fog lights
   d. full headlights

28 Fog lights should be used when:
   a. you need to use headlights
   b. you drive in rural areas at night
   c. your visibility is seriously reduced
   d. visibility is less than 100 metres

29 In wet weather your tyres:
    a. have less grip on the road
    b. have more grip on the road
    c. need to be inflated to a higher pressure
    d. need to be inflated to a lower pressure

30 Before driving away in icy conditions you should:
    a. clear a patch in the windscreen
    b. clear the front and side windows
    c. clear all of the windows
    d. de-mist the windows thoroughly.

You will find the answers on page 223

Scores: 1st try ☐ ; 2nd try ☐ ; 3rd try ☐ .

Record your scores in the appendix on page 225.

Driving at higher speeds, simple mechanics and dealing with emergencies

Introduction

When you can drive confidently in most of the situations covered in the previous eight stages, your instructor should teach you how to drive safely at higher speeds. You may have to take longer lessons to get to areas where there are dual carriageways that carry the national speed limit. Driving on this type of road will prepare you for motorway driving, as it is very similar.

Although as a learner you are not allowed to drive on motorways, you do need to know the rules. Not only will this prepare you for your theory test, but it will mean that as soon as you have passed the test you will be able to apply those rules.

It is your responsibility as a driver to ensure the car you are driving is roadworthy. Although this will not really apply to the driving school car as your instructor should take good care of it, it will matter when you are practising in your own vehicle.

You should know how to carry out simple tasks including:

- checking tyre pressures and tread;

- changing wheels;

- checking oil and water levels;

- replacing bulbs.

You will be asked questions on these and other vehicle checks in the theory test. You should also know what to do in cases of breakdowns and other emergencies.

Before going out to practise, read sections 11, 14, 15 and 16 of **The Driving Manual**, and Annex B in the **Highway Code** entitled: 'Vehicle maintenance, safety and security'; and 'First aid on the road'.

Learn the following **Highway Code** rules:

227–247 Motorways
248–261 Breakdowns and accidents
262–264 Roadworks

Planning your journeys

Avoid frustration by
starting out early

During your final preparation for your practical driving test you should learn how to read and follow road signs. This should help prepare you for driving alone after you have passed. Here are some tips for preparing for a journey:

Allow yourself plenty of time: in today's congested traffic you cannot depend on getting to your destination in the shortest possible time. The later you are, the more frustrated you will become to the point where you may even be tempted to take risks.

Plan your journey: organize yourself with a route plan, noting down all the road numbers and names of towns. Start out early, making sure you allow time for roadworks and other problems. A route card only takes a few minutes to prepare and if you have a computer you can get programmes which give you the best routes.

Keep your concentration to a maximum: If you are going a long distance take plenty of breaks. Keep the temperature comfortable and not too stuffy. Only listen to light programmes on the radio or music centre. Remember, fiddling about with discs and tapes can be a distraction while you are driving.

Mobile phones: In emergencies, mobile phones can be extremely useful (particularly if you are a lone female driver). Remember however, they should only be used while you are stationary.

Lane discipline

When you drive on any type of dual carriageway or motorway, make sure you keep to the correct lane. Many of the hold-ups that occur on these roads are caused by people not driving in the left lane when it is reasonably clear. Remember, on a three-lane motorway you should use the:

- **left lane** for normal driving unless there are a number of slower moving vehicles – you may then use the centre lane;

- **centre lane** as above but return to the left lane when clear;

- **right lane** for overtaking only.

Look and plan well ahead, using your mirrors to keep aware of what is happening all around all of the time. Work out in good time whether the traffic ahead in the left and centre lanes is moving more slowly and you need to consider overtaking. This will allow you more thinking time after checking the mirrors to work out whether or not your manoeuvre will be safe.

Anticipate drivers ahead preparing to overtake and be prepared to act. You may either slow down a little or, if safe, move over to the next lane on your right. Expect people to be joining the motorway from slip roads and, if you have time and it is safe, be prepared to move over to allow them on to the main carriageway.

When approaching your exit, look for the signs and plan ahead so that you can get over in good time without causing problems for other drivers. Remember that the deceleration lane is for slowing down. Unless there are queues for your exit, try not to slow down drivers on the motorway.

Speed can be deceiving. Once in the deceleration lane keep checking your speed and make sure you have full control as you approach the junction.

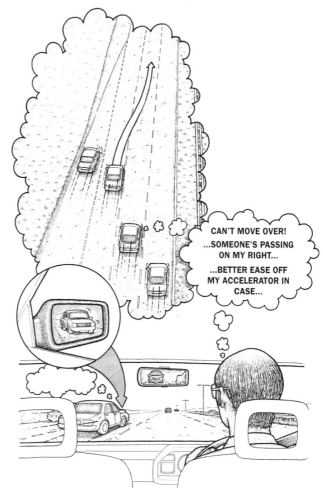

Using the mirrors

Reducing the risk of breakdowns

Your car should be maintained in a roadworthy condition. This will reduce the chances of your being involved in breakdowns and accidents. Before driving, take a look around your vehicle for any obvious defects.

Weekly checks

P – Petrol. Or whatever fuel your vehicle runs on. Try to avoid running on less than a quarter tank. Check your fuel as soon as you switch on. Remember if you are travelling far, it may be a long way to the next service station.

O – Oil. Check the engine oil and the brake fluid. Look for tell-tale drips under the car. If the oil pressure, or brake warning, light comes on while driving, stop as soon as it is safe and check the problem out. If you run your engine without oil, it could seize up.

W – Water. Make sure there is water in the washer bottle. When the engine is cold, check the radiator coolant. In the winter check for anti-freeze, although many cars now have sealed units and this may not be necessary.

E – Electrics. Before driving, check that all the lights and indicators are working. Keep spare bulbs in the car. Check that the electrolyte fluid level in the battery covers the plates. If necessary top this up with distilled water.

R – Rubber. Check the tyre pressures and look for any obvious cuts or bulges. Remove any stones from the tread. You could get a puncture at any time, so check the spare as well. Check that the fan belt is tight and that it's not fraying. If the wiper blades smear the screen get them changed.

Check the POWER

Changing a wheel

When changing a wheel as a matter of routine, you should park on level, firm ground. Put on the handbrake and leave the car in gear. If you are on the road switch on your hazard flashers and, if you have one, place your warning triangle at least 45 metres behind your car on the same side of the road. Unfortunately, you never know when or where you will get a puncture. If you are on a slope, position a brick or heavy object at each side of one of the good wheels to prevent movement. Be aware of other traffic and try not to stand in front of your lights at night.

Changing a wheel

Place the spare wheel, jack and wheel brace (spanner) near the tyre to be changed. Slightly loosen the wheelnuts of the flat tyre. If these are difficult to turn you may have to use your foot and bodyweight on the lever. Make sure you support yourself as you do this so that you are not injured.

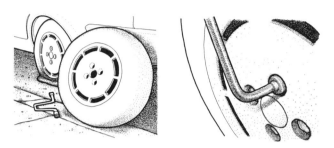

Position the jack under a solid part of the vehicle. Most cars now have special jacking points that will be illustrated in the car's handbook. Now raise the vehicle enough to allow room for the properly inflated tyre to be fitted.

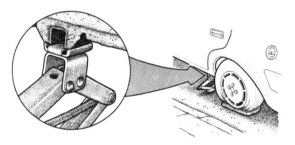

Remove the wheelnuts and take off the wheel.

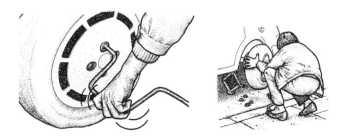

Fit the new wheel locating two opposite nuts finger tight. Fit the other nuts and tighten them all lightly with the brace.

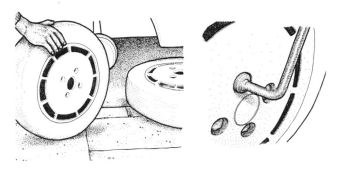

Lower the jack and tighten the nuts as much as possible.

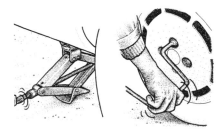

Remove the chocks and remember to replace the tools and the flat tyre in the boot. Check the pressure of the replacement tyre as soon as possible.

If you break down

If possible, try not to inconvenience others and get your car off the road. Switch on your hazard flashers and place your warning triangle 45 metres behind the car on the same side of the road. At night, be careful not to stand in front of your lights. If you are a lone female, in quieter areas lock yourself in the car and be prepared to speak to others through a slightly open window.

If you don't have a mobile phone and there is no-one around, you may have to walk for assistance yourself. Make sure you lock the car, putting any valuables in the boot.

In cases of emergency the police and motoring organizations give priority to lone women.

Before setting out on a long journey, it can be useful to let someone know your route, destination and estimated time of arrival.

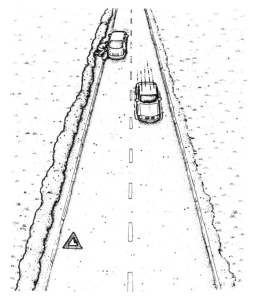

Place a warning triangle about 50 metres from your vehicle (Except on a motorway)

If you break down on a motorway

If your car develops a problem try to get it to the next exit or service area. If you can't do this you should:

- get over to the hard shoulder as safely as possible and stop as far to the left as you can with your wheels turned to the left;

- try to stop near one of the emergency telephones;

- if you have a disability and can't get out of the car, display a 'help' sign and wait for the police;

- you and your passengers should exit to the nearside;

- unless there is a real emergency, leave animals in the car;

- do not try to 'fix it' – you are putting yourself in danger;

- make sure all passengers get as far away from the carriageway and hard shoulder as possible;

- keep children, and animals, under control;

- walk to the nearest emergency telephone. An arrow on the post will tell you which way this is. This is a free service and you will get quicker response than by using a mobile;

- give full details and inform the operator if you are a lone woman;

- go back and wait on the verge near your vehicle;

- should you feel threatened by someone, get in your car from the left and lock the doors. If the danger passes, get out and on to the verge again.

What to do at the scene of an accident

You never know when you're going to arrive at the scene of an accident. Could you do anything to help or would you be one of those who just stands and stares?

Keep your first aid kit where it will be easy to get at. If you get to the scene before anyone else, keep calm. Take charge until someone else better qualified arrives. Either call yourself or get someone else to phone for the emergency services.

People with injuries should be kept warm and reassure them by talking to them. Do not give them anything to eat or drink.

Some knowledge of first aid can be very helpful – you could save a life by following some of the simple procedures outlined in Part 16 of **The Driving Manual** and in the annex of the **Highway Code**.

If you'd like to better equip yourself for dealing with anyone injured in an accident, the St John Ambulance service runs courses all over the country – look in your Yellow Pages.

Reducing the risk of fire

Although the risk of fire in modern cars is minimal, it is sensible to carry a fire extinguisher.

Pipes can become damaged in accidents and fuel could leak on to electrical contacts. The engine of any vehicle involved should be switched off immediately.

If no-one else has done so, impose a 'no-smoking' rule at the scene. If you suspect your car may have electrical problems, get it checked as soon as possible.

Emergency vehicles

If you are planning well ahead and checking your mirrors regularly you should know when an emergency vehicle is approaching.

As soon as you hear sirens, check what is happening all around, look to see which direction the vehicle is travelling in and be ready to pull in to let it by.

Sometimes emergency vehicles are travelling through traffic light controlled junctions in a hurry – remember 'Green means go only if it is safe!' Someone's life may be at stake.

Vehicle security

The theft of vehicles and their contents has now become extremely common. To reduce the risk make sure you secure your car and its contents properly. You should:

- close all windows and sunroofs;

- retract aerials where possible;

- use a 'krook-lock';

- put valuables in the boot;

- remove the keys while in filling stations;

- get your windows etched with the registration number;

- get an immobilizer fitted;

- buy only coded audio equipment;

- use lockable fuel caps and wheel nuts if possible.

Park your car in well lit areas if possible. If you are leaving a window open for a pet, it is sensible to fit a grille into the gap to deter any would-be thief.

Be alert: if you see anyone acting suspiciously around another vehicle, call the police.

Checkpoint

1 If you become tired while driving you should:
   a. open a window
   b. stop when safe to rest
   c. pull over to the hard shoulder
   d. stop when safe to have a soft drink

2 Motorways must not be used by riders of motorcycles:
   a. under 50 cc
   b. over 50 cc
   c. under 125 but over 125 cc
   d. over 125 cc

3 Red reflective studs mark the:
   a. right edge of the road
   b. left edge of the road
   c. centre of motorways
   d. motorway entry slip roads

4 It is more difficult to judge the speed and distance of other traffic:
   a. at dusk
   b. if you wear glasses
   c. in the interior mirror
   d. in the exterior mirror

5 You may overtake on the left:
   a. on one-way streets
   b. when turning left at a junction
   c. on two-lane motorways
   d. in lanes of slow moving traffic

6 You must not overtake unless:
   a. you can see for at least 50 metres
   b. you can see the road ahead is clear
   c. other drivers are overtaking
   d. it is necessary

7 You should not normally overtake:
   a   on two-lane highways
   b. near junctions
   c. on the left on dual carriageways
   d. if there is dead ground ahead

8 You should not overtake:
   a. in a built-up area
   b. on any country roads
   c. approaching a hazard line
   d. near single broken lines

9 You should use the motorway slip road to:
   a. build up your speed
   b. look for a gap in the traffic
   c. change into 5th gear
   d. check over your left shoulder

10 When joining a motorway you should be travelling at:
   a. 50 mph
   b   60 mph
   c. 70 mph
   d. the speed of the traffic in the left lane of the main
       carriageway

11 Learner drivers must not:
   a. use dual carriageways
   b. use motorways
   c. drive up to 70 mph
   d. drive at less than 20 mph

12 To leave a motorway you should:
   a. keep a lookout for the signs
   b. move to the left lane as soon as you see the 300 yard
       marker
   c. move to the left lane well before reaching the exit
       markers
   d. slow down as soon as you see the half mile marker

13 If something falls from your car while you are on a
    motorway you should:
   a. stop on the hard shoulder and retrieve it
   b. stop on the hard shoulder and telephone the police
   c. leave at the next exit and telephone the police
   d. consider it irretrievable and forget about it

14 Flashing red lights above your lane on a motorway mean:
   a. do not proceed further in that lane
   b. leave the motorway at the next exit
   c. move over to the next lane quickly
   d. the next light will be steady amber

15 Motorways may be used by:
   a. agricultural vehicles at harvest time
   b. three-wheeled cars
   c. invalid carriages with an orange badge
   d. vehicles carrying oversized loads

16 If you break down on a two-lane road you should first
    of all:
   a. telephone for the breakdown service
   b. think of other traffic
   c. get your passengers out
   d. call home on your mobile phone

17 If you are driving on a motorway and think there may be a problem with your car you should first of all:
   a. use your mobile phone to call the police
   b. try to get over to the hard shoulder
   c. get your passengers out of the car
   d. telephone for the breakdown service

18 Anxiety and frustration can be reduced by:
   a. starting your journey earlier
   b. keeping the air conditioning on
   c. taking anti-depressants
   d. accepting that you will sometimes be held up in traffic queues

19 If you break down on a two-lane highway you should place a warning triangle:
   a. at least 45 metres behind your car
   b. at least 45 metres ahead of your car
   c. on the opposite side of the road
   d. on the same side of the road

20 If you break down on a motorway you should:
   a. place a warning triangle at least 100 metres behind your car
   b. not use a warning triangle
   c. switch on the hazard warning lights
   d. switch on the fog lights at night

21 When wishing to leave a motorway which is carrying freely moving traffic you should slow down:
   a. as soon as you see the half mile sign
   b. as soon as you see the 300 yard marker
   c. as soon as you move into the left lane
   d. when you move into the slip road

22 When you see a sign for road works you:
   a. may exceed the temporary speed limit
   b. must not exceed the temporary speed limit
   c. may switch lanes to get into a shorter queue
   d. may go through a red light at night if there is no oncoming traffic

23 If you're involved in an accident causing damage to property or injury to someone you must:
 a. drive straight to a police station to report the incident
 b. stop
 c give your name and address to anyone with grounds for requiring them
 d. give the registration number and the name of the owner to anyone with grounds for requiring them

24 If you cannot produce your insurance certificate at the time of an accident which involves injury, you must produce it for the police within:
 a. 24 hours
 b. two days
 c. five days
 d. seven days

25 If a vehicle containing a flammable load is involved in an accident you should:
 a. switch off engines to avoid sparks
 b. not switch off engines because of sparks
 c. use a mobile phone to call for help
 d. not use a mobile phone

26 If you get a puncture in a tyre while driving you should:
 a. brake as quickly as you can
 b. don't brake suddenly
 c. steer over to the left
 d. try to keep the car straight

27 If the oil pressure warning light shows while you are driving you should:
 a. drive home immediately
 b. drive to the nearest garage
 c. stop as soon as it is safe
 d. check the oil level

28 If using a mix of two radial and two crossply tyres you should fit the radials to the:
 a. front wheels
 b. rear wheels
 c. nearside wheels
 d. offside wheels

29 You should run in new tyres at reasonable speeds for the first:
   a. 100 miles
   b. 75 miles
   c. 50 miles
   d. 25 miles

30 If someone is injured in an accident and they stop breathing you should:
   a. tilt their head towards the window
   b. tilt their head backwards
   c. tilt their head forwards
   d. pinch their nose and blow into their mouth

You will find the answers on page 224

Scores: 1st try ☐ ; 2nd try ☐ ; 3rd try ☐ .

Record your scores in the appendix on page 225.

The driving test and the Pass Plus scheme

The driving test

When you have passed the theory test, you should be able to concentrate on putting all of the rules you have learnt into practice in preparation for your practical test.

If you have had enough driving lessons and plenty of practice, you should be able to carry out with confidence all of the skills outlined in Section 2 of the DSA book **The Driving Test**.

Applying for the test

It is important that you complete the application form under the guidance of your instructor. This will help ensure:

- it is completed properly and so avoid any delays;

- you don't get an appointment before you're ready;

- your instructor doesn't have another test at the same time.

Before you attend for your test

If you need an interpreter to attend with you, ensure you make arrangements in good time.

Before the test

A few lessons prior to the test, your instructor will probably conduct a couple of 'mock' tests. This will:

- ensure that you can still read a number from 20.5 metres;

- demonstrate what it's like to drive totally unaided;

- ensure that you both know you can deal with hazards effectively without any help;

- show up any weaknesses in your knowledge or skills.

If your instructor still has to give you help – you will not be ready to cope on your own, either during or after the test. If this is the case, it is advisable to postpone your test. You must give the DSA at least 10 clear working days' notice. Otherwise, you will lose the fee.

Arriving at the test centre

When your instructor picks you up on the day of your test, make sure that you have:

- the appointment card;

- your driving licence;

- your theory test pass certificate;

- photographic identification such as your passport.

Your instructor will make sure that you arrive early, leaving plenty of time to park and relax. Tell your instructor in good time if you wish to use the toilet. Some test centres do not have facilities.

It is natural for test candidates to feel a little anxious. Don't worry, your instructor wouldn't let you attempt it if you were not ready!

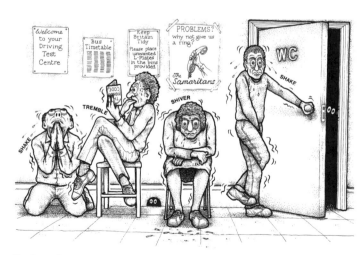

Test centre nerves

The test

Your examiner will ask you to sign a form. Your signature will be checked against that on your diving licence and other means of identification.

If you wish your instructor to sit in the car for the test, ask the examiner at this point. You will be asked whether you have any physical disabilities not declared in your application form. Sometimes senior examiners have to accompany driving examiners on tests. This is to ensure uniformity is maintained. Try to relax and remember that the examiner is being checked by this person, not you.

Before you get into the car you will be asked to read a number plate. Remember you may feel a little flustered. This could affect how you see the letters and numbers. Take your time.

While you make sure it is safe and get in, the examiner will look around to make sure the car looks roadworthy.

During the test

The examiner will explain the instructions that will be given. Unless you are asked to turn left or right, you should follow the road ahead or go in the direction of any signs or markings. Remember this is all part of the test. The examiner is checking that you can read and follow signs on your own. If you see a 'turn left' or 'turn right' sign obey it. Don't be tempted to ask which way to go.

During the first few minutes, the examiner should give you time to settle down. Try to relax and concentrate on what is happening on the road all around rather than wondering what the person sitting by your side is thinking.

Put everything into practice that your instructor has taught you. Show how confident you can be. Don't try to be over-careful but take all safe opportunities to proceed. However, if you are at all in doubt – hold back.

Planning ahead

Show how well you can drive by:

- looking and planning well ahead;

- making good use of all of the mirrors;

- showing discrimination in the use and timing of signals;

- concentrating on what is happening all around;

- adjusting your speed well before you reach any hazards by using all of the controls gently;

- allowing adequate clearance and safety margins;

- showing care and consideration to all other road users;

- anticipating and making allowance for others' mistakes.

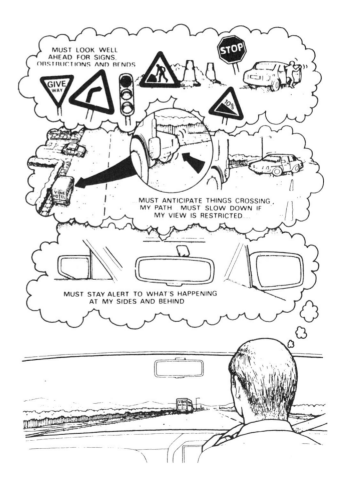

Make proper progress, you will not impress your examiner by being over-cautious!

Over-caution could lead to failure

The manoeuvre exercises

During the test you will be asked to pull in on the left. This is also part of the test. Make sure you stop where it is safe, legal and convenient. If you are asked to pull in behind another vehicle – make sure you leave plenty of room for moving away again.

As well as making normal stops you may be asked to carry out an emergency stop. You will also be asked to carry out a number of the following exercises:

- reverse to the left or right (particularly if you are in a van);

- turn the car round in the road;

- reverse park.

You should have had plenty of practice at all of these exercises. Remember the things your examiner will be looking for are good control, accuracy, and all-round observations.

Control

Work out what sort of gradient you are on so that you'll know whether to control the speed with the gas and clutch or with the brake. Keep the speed down so that you have full control of the steering wheel and plenty of time to keep checking for others. Maintain full control throughout and use the handbrake when necessary.

Accuracy

Keeping the speed down should help you carry out all of the exercises efficiently. Make sure you finish all of the reversing exercises in a safe place.

Observations

Your observations, and how you respond to other road users, are just as important as your control and accuracy. Remember – when you are manoeuvring, others have priority.

At the end of the test

When you return to the test centre, your examiner will complete a Driving Test Report Form. This will show those items on which you made mistakes. Not all mistakes result in failure, only those which were serious or dangerous, or if you accumulate more than 15 driver faults. Your examiner will offer you a verbal explanation. Your instructor may be present for this.

Your instructor will probably drive you home. This is normal. You will be either too excited or too disappointed to concentrate properly.

After passing

You are more likely to pass first time if you have plenty of lessons. Take your instructor's advice and only take your test when you are ready.

Send off for your full licence as soon as possible. This will permit you to drive anywhere in Europe and in some other countries. Check on the Form D100 for further details.

If you try to continually improve your driving skills, you will find that you get many years of enjoyment from your newly acquired freedom of travel.

If you fail

Those items you have failed for will be marked on the Driving Test Report Form and the examiner will explain these to you.

Don't worry about failing. You may not have been ready to be out on your own after all. Your instructor will advise you on any further training requirements before you take another test.

It is important that you keep up with your lessons so that the standard you have reached doesn't fall.

The Pass Plus scheme

By passing the test you have shown that you can drive to the minimum standard required by law. You are now only at the beginning of your real driving career. You should be prepared to continue learning for a long time to come. To help you with this your instructor will be able to advise you on the elements in the Pass Plus scheme which will be of benefit and which you may not have covered during your driving lessons. It will also help reduce the risk of your being involved in a road accident.

It is far better to gain experience in different conditions and on different roads, particularly motorways, under the expert and safe guidance of a professional before you try to take on too much too soon.

The subjects covered in the Pass Plus scheme include driving on motorways; at night; in rural areas; and in different weather conditions.

Passed!

Throughout the course you will be driving with these key factors in mind:

Attitude: responsibility for your actions and care and consideration for others.

Skills: observation; assessing what you see; taking the right action.

Some insurance companies offer discounts to drivers who have taken extra training under this scheme. Ask your instructor for details.

Advanced driving tests

If you are really interested in continually improving your standard of driving you might consider taking one of the advanced driving tests offered by either The Royal Society for the Prevention of Accidents – RoSPA (tel: 0121 248 2000); or The Institute of Advanced Motorists – IAM (tel: 0181 994 4403).

> Congratulations!
> I hope you have found this book useful and that it has made your driving lessons easier and enjoyable. You will get some more useful tips on improving your skills from my other book *The Advanced Driver's Handbook*.
> Margaret Stacey

By the time you apply for your theory test you should be able to answer the questions in all of the other checkpoints. Your instructor should have been teaching you how to put all of the rules and procedures into practice.

Remember – you are not learning these rules just in order to pass your test! You need to understand them so that you can apply them and enjoy 'safe driving for life'.

This checkpoint includes questions which cover all of the syllabus for learning and also other general rules for all drivers.

Checkpoint

1 The main items inspected on an MOT test are:
   a. engine, gearbox, brakes and tyres
   b. brakes, lights, steering and tyres
   c. engine, body, brakes and tyres
   d. paintwork, metal trims, body and tyres

2 You should check your engine oil:
   a. before every journey
   b. at least once a week
   c. once a month
   d. at service intervals

3 Lights and indicators should be checked:
   a. before you drive
   b. once a week
   c. once a month
   d. at service intervals

4 Before driving you should check the:
   a. radiator coolant
   b. horn is working
   c. windscreen washer level
   d. gearbox fluid level

5 The main cause of skidding is:
   a. a wet road surface
   b. icy roads
   c. high speed
   d. the driver

6 When you attend for your practical driving test you should take with you:
   a. your application form
   b. your appointment card
   c. your driving licence
   d. some photographic identification

7 If the rear of your car is skidding to the left you should
   a. brake more firmly
   b. pump the brake on and off
   c. steer to the right
   d. steer to the left

8 If your wheels lock up during an emergency stop you should:
   a. brake more firmly
   b. use the handbrake to help
   c. release the brake and re-apply it
   d. push down the clutch

9 Tyres must be:
   a. all radial
   b. all crossply
   c. a mix of crossply and radial
   d. free of defects

10 Tyres must have a tread depth of:
   a. 1.6 mm across the central three quarters of the width
   b. 1.6 mm across the entire width
   c. 2.00 mm across the central three quarters of the width
   d. 2.00 mm across the entire width

11 You may proceed through a steady amber light if:
   a. no-one is crossing your path
   b. it is safe to do so
   c. you are too close to stop safely
   d. you have crossed the stop line

12 You may proceed through a flashing amber light if:
   a. there is no-one on the crossing
   b. you are sure no-one will step out
   c. you use your horn to warn people nearby
   d. a pedestrian beckons you on

13 Flashing amber at a pelican crossing means:
   a. proceed but clear the crossing quickly
   b. give way to all pedestrians within 100 metres
   c. give way to all pedestrians waiting to cross
   d. only go if the crossing is clear

14 On the approach to a zebra crossing you should:
   a. be travelling at a speed at which you can stop safely
   b. be ready to stop
   c. check your mirrors early
   d. only stop when someone steps out

15 At zebra crossings special consideration should be given to:
  a. the very old
  b. the very young
  c. people with prams
  d. people with shopping bags

16 If you see a person with a guide dog waiting to cross the road you should:
  a. always wait for them
  b. proceed carefully
  c. wave them across
  d. sound your horn to warn them of your presence

17 Driving past parked vehicles you should should look for:
  a. pedestrians walking out
  b. car doors opening
  c. hidden entrances
  d. high-sided vehicles

18 So as not to frighten animals you should be ready to:
  a. slow down
  b. sound the horn to warn them
  c. drive past quickly out of danger
  d. keep the engine speed low

19 If you are turning into a road where there are pedestrians you should:
  a. sound the horn
  b. give way to them
  c. wave them across
  d. don't rush them

20 You are approaching the end of a road and there are pedestrians crossing, you should:
  a. hold back for them
  b. expect them to wait
  c. sound the horn
  d. flash your lights

21 You may sound the horn when stationary on the road:
  a. to test it
  b. when in danger from another car
  c. between 7.00 am and 11.00 pm
  d. at no time

22 You should not sound your horn in built-up areas between the hours of:
   a. 10.30 pm and 7.30 pm
   b. 7.30 am and 10.30 pm
   c. 11.30 pm and 7.00 am
   d. 7.00 am and 11.30 pm

23 If another driver makes a mistake you should:
   a. flash your lights
   b. sound your horn
   c. be ready to compensate
   d. shake your head

24 If there is a solid white line along the centre of your side of the road it means:
   a. no overtaking on that road
   b. you should not cross the line
   c. you should not park on the offside
   d. you may only overtake a vehicle travelling at less than 10 mph

25 A broken yellow line along the left edge of the road means:
   a. no waiting at any time
   b. waiting is prohibited
   c. no waiting at weekends
   d. loading is not permitted

26 Box junctions are normally marked with:
   a. a white box and yellow diagonals
   b. a yellow box and white diagonals
   c. a yellow box and yellow diagonals
   d. a white box and white diagonals

27 Overtaking is not allowed when:
   a. driving on two-lane highways
   b. driving in built-up areas
   c. near junctions
   d. on rural roads

28 Countdown markers are usually found on the approach to:
   a. motorway exits
   b. some roundabouts
   c. some deceleration lanes
   d. all railway level crossings

29 Countdown markers on motorways are:
   a. white on black
   b. black on white
   c. blue on white
   d. white on blue

30 Countdown markers for roundabouts are normally:
   a. white on green
   b. green on white
   c. yellow on green
   d. green on yellow

31 Countdown markers may indicate the distance to a:
   a. motorway entrance
   b. motorway exit
   c. a concealed level crossing
   d. hazard

32 Round signs usually give:
   a. orders
   b. warnings
   c. information
   d. directions

33 Triangular signs usually give:
   a. orders
   b. warnings
   c. information
   d. instructions

34 Red circles usually tell you:
   a. not to do something
   b. to do something
   c. maximum speed limits
   d. minimum speed limits

35 Blue circles usually tell you:
   a. not to do something
   b. to do something
   c. maximum speed limits
   d. minimum speed limits

36 At mini-roundabouts you should:
   a. give way to traffic from the right
   b. give way to all other traffic
   c. beware of vehicles making U turns
   d. expect drivers to your left to give way to you

37 When turning right at a roundabout you should:
   a. keep on the right signal throughout the manoeuvre
   b. signal left after you have passed the exit before yours
   c. signal left before you pass the exit before yours
   d. stay in the left lane all the way for safety

38 Dead ground is a road with:
   a. hidden hollows
   b. a non-slip surface
   c. a crematorium
   d. a ban on traffic

39 If you use full beam headlights at the wrong time you could:
   a. dazzle oncoming drivers
   b. dazzle the driver in front
   c. be seen more clearly
   d. burn out more bulbs

40 If you don't use all of your mirrors regularly when you drive on motorways you could:
   a. be paying more attention to what is happening to your sides
   b. be unaware of safe gaps to use when you wish to overtake
   c. be unaware of drivers in your blind areas
   d. avoid fatigue on long journeys

41 Following another vehicle at night you should use:
   a. dipped headlights
   b. sidelights
   c. fog lights only
   d. rear fog lights only

42 The camber is the angle at which the road slopes:
   a. towards the centre
   b. away from the centre.
   This helps:
   c. drainage
   d. with steering

43 Adverse camber is where the road slopes to the:
  a. outer edge of a bend
  b. inner edge of a bend
  This helps:
  c. you maintain a high speed
  d. with roadholding

44 Before manoeuvring you should ask yourself if it is:
  a. safe
  b. convenient
  c. lawful
  d. too wide a road

45 A person who is supervising a learner driver must have held a full driving licence for:
  a. at least three years
  b. at least two years
  For:
  c. any category of vehicle
  d. the category of vehicle being driven

46 The major cause of 'L' test failure is not:
  a. being properly prepared
  b. passing the theory test first
  c. having private practice
  d. applying early enough

47 To make sure there is enough time for your test, when you apply you should declare whether you:
  a. have severe hearing difficulties
  b. are restricted in your movements
  c. have any disabilities which may affect your driving
  d. have had professional tuition

48 During your driving test you should drive:
  a. perfectly
  b. like a learner
  c. as an experienced driver
  d. to suit the road and traffic conditions

49 When preparing for your driving test you should practise:
  a. on test routes only
  b. on as many types of road as possible
  c. in all sorts of conditions
  d. in daylight only

50 If you pass your test in an automatic car you:
  a. may only drive automatic cars
  b. will have to take a test in a manual car within two years
  c. may drive any type of automatic vehicle
  d. may not drive any left-hand drive vehicle

You will find the answers on page 224

Scores: 1st try [   ] ; 2nd try [   ] ; 3rd try [   ]

Record your scores in the appendix on page 225.

Answers to checkpoints

Checkpoint 1

1	b	**11**	b	**21**	c
2	d	**12**	a	**22**	a, c, d, e
3	d	**13**	b	**23**	b, c
4	d	**14**	a, b	**24**	b
5	c	**15**	d	**25**	a, b
6	b	**16**	c	**26**	b
7	c	**17**	a, e	**27**	b, d
8	d	**18**	c	**28**	d
9	d	**19**	a, b	**29**	a
10	b	**20**	b, c, d	**30**	c

Checkpoint 2

1	a, b, d	**11**	a, c, e	**21**	a
2	a, b, d	**12**	a	**22**	b
3	a, b	**13**	a, b, c	**23**	a
4	b, c	**14**	c	**24**	b
5	b, c	**15**	a, d	**25**	a, c
6	a, d	**16**	a, b	**26**	a, c
7	b, c	**17**	a	**27**	a
8	b, c, d	**18**	c	**28**	a, b
9	a, d, e	**19**	c	**29**	a, c, d
10	b, c	**20**	a, c	**30**	a, b

Checkpoint 3

1	a	11	a, b, c	21	a, b
2	b	12	b	22	d
3	a	13	b	23	a, b
4	c, d	14	a, b, d	24	b, c
5	a, b, c	15	a, b, c	25	c, d
6	b, c	16	c	26	b, c, d
7	b, c	17	a, b, c	27	a, d
8	a	18	a, b, d	28	a, b, d
9	a	19	c	29	b, d
10	a	20	c	30	a

Checkpoint 4

1	a	11	a	21	b, c
2	b	12	c	22	a, b
3	d	13	b, d	23	c, d
4	b	14	a	24	a, b, d
5	d	15	c	25	b, c, d
6	c	16	a, d	26	a, b, c
7	c	17	a, b, d	27	b, c, d
8	b	18	b, c, d	28	a, d
9	b, d	19	a, c	29	d
10	a, c	20	b, c	30	a, b, c, d, e

Checkpoint 5

1	b	11	a	21	a
2	b	12	b, c, d	22	d
3	a	13	a, b	23	b, c, d
4	b	14	c	24	c, d
5	c	15	b	25	b, c
6	c	16	b, d	26	a, c, d
7	d	17	b	27	b, c
8	c	18	c	28	b, c
9	b, d	19	c	29	d
10	c	20	d	30	a, c, d

Checkpoint 6

1	b	9	a,	17	a, b, d
2	b	10	a	18	c
3	a	11	b, d	19	b, d
4	b	12	c, d	20	a
5	b, d	13	d	21	b, d
6	b, c	14	a, b	22	a, c
7	b	15	b, c	23	a, b, d
8	a, d	16	a, d	24	b, d

Checkpoint 7

1	c, d	11	a, d	21	a, d
2	b, c	12	b	22	b, c
3	a, d	13	a	23	b
4	a	14	c	24	b, d
5	a	15	a, d	25	a, c
6	a, c	16	b	26	b
7	a, b, d	17	b	27	b, c
8	b	18	a, b	28	d
9	a	19	a, d	29	b, d
10	b	20	b, d	30	b, c

Checkpoint 8

1	b, d	11	b, c	21	b
2	b	12	a, d	22	c
3	c	13	b, d	23	a, b
4	a, d	14	b	24	b, c, d
5	b, d	15	b, d	25	a, c
6	c	16	a, c, d	26	a, b, d
7	b, c	17	b, c, d	27	a
8	a, b, c	18	a, c, d	28	c, d
9	b, d	19	b, c	29	a
10	a, d	20	a	30	c, d

Checkpoint 9

1	a, b, d	11	b	21	d
2	a	12	a, c	22	b
3	b	13	b	23	b, c, d
4	a, d	14	a	24	d
5	a, b, d	15	b, d	25	a, d
6	b, d	16	b	26	b, d
7	b, c, d	17	b	27	c, d
8	c	18	a, d	28	b
9	a	19	a, d	29	a
10	d	20	b, c	30	b, d

Checkpoint 10

1	b	18	a, d	35	b, d
2	b	19	b, d	36	a, c
3	a	20	a	37	b
4	b, c	21	b	38	a
5	d	22	c	39	a, b
6	b, c, d	23	c	40	b, c
7	b, d	24	b, d	41	a
8	c	25	b	42	b, c
9	d	26	c	43	a, d
10	a	27	c	44	a, b, c
11	c, d	28	a, b, c	45	a, d
12	a, b	29	d	46	a
13	d	30	a	47	a, b, c
14	a, b, c	31	b, c, d	48	d
15	a, b, c	32	a	49	b, c
16	b	33	b	50	a
17	a, b, c	34	a, c		

Checkpoint scores

This section of **Learn to Drive in 10 Easy Stages** is designed to help you build up a picture of your progress. It should help you understand whether you are ready to apply for your driving test or highlight any areas that need further revision and practice.

It is in you own interest not to cheat. You should have answered the questions at the end of each Stage honestly. This will show where there are any weaknesses in your knowledge.

Your instructor or supervisor should also have been frequently checking by asking you questions on the rules and regulations.

As you complete the checkpoint at the end of each Stage, record your scores below. If you cannot answer all of the questions, revise those you are not sure about and try again.

Stage	1st Try	2nd Try	3rd Try
1	☐	☐	☐
2	☐	☐	☐
3	☐	☐	☐
4	☐	☐	☐
5	☐	☐	☐
6	☐	☐	☐
7	☐	☐	☐
8	☐	☐	☐
9	☐	☐	☐
10	☐	☐	☐

'Can do' statements

The driving test is designed so candidates will be able to show they can drive competently and safely, making decisions that will ensure their own safely and that of other road users.

The 'Can do' statements should help you understand and measure your learning achievements. Learning about the rules should help you to make sensible decisions. Your confidence and ability should grow with plenty of practice.

There are three stages in learning to drive. To begin with your instructor will control your actions and tell you exactly what to do. As you improve, your instructor should only need to give you prompts, sometimes hust by asking a question. Finally your ability and confidence should have developed so much that all your instructor has to do is check on your performance and give any corrective advice necessary. This is the stage when the responsibility for making decisions has been passed to you and you should be ready for taking your driving test.

You might feel self-assessment is too much bother! However, to get the best value from your training, you will need to be aware of your successes and failures. This will show you where progress is being achieved. You may be surprised to discover that your own marking would not differ too greatly from your instructor's

As you tick the boxes throughout the text of this book, fill in the dates on the 'Can do' statements table to chart your progress at each lesson or practice session.

Subject	Talk through	Prompted	Unaided
Starting precautions			
Make proper use of: accelerator clucth gears footbrake handbrake steering			
Move off safely			
Emergency stop			
Reverse left			
Reverse right			
Turn in the road			
Reverse park			
Use of mirrors			
Use of signals			
Act on signs/signals			
Making progress			
T Junctions: M S M speed on approach observations position/left position/right position/ahead			
Crossroads: M S M speed on approach observations position/right position/left			
Roundabouts: M S M speed on approach observations position/right position/left			
Meet others			
Safety clearances			
Crossing path of others			
Pedestrian crossings			
Overtaking			
Dual carriageways			
Railway crossings			
Parking			
Anticipating: pedestrians cyclists other drivers			

Tick the appropriate column and make a note of the dates until you improve to the point where you can carry out most of the skills without any help.

227

Driving test analysis and revision

Use the following list and page references to help organise your revision. The numbers on the left correspond to those on the Driving Test Report Form:

1(a) Eyesight: **Learn to Drive**, page 12; **The Driving Test**, page 19.

1(b) Highway Code: **The Driving Test**, page 20.

2 Precautions: **Learn to Drive**, page 21; **The Driving Test**, page 21.

3 Control:
accelerator: **Learn to Drive**, pages 28, 51, 52; **The Driving Test**, pages 22, 23.
clutch: **Learn to Drive**, pages 18, 29, 30, 50, 51, 52, 53; **The Driving Test**, pages 23, 24.
gears: **Learn to Drive**, pages 26, 27, 39, 40, 54, 55; **The Driving Test**, page 24.
footbrake: **Learn to Drive**, pages 27, 28, 42, 43, 44, 56, 57, 58; **The Driving Test**, pages 23, 24.
handbrake: **Learn to Drive**, pages 23; **The Driving Test**, page 24.
steering: **Learn to Drive**, pages 12, 19, 20, 24, 25, 41, 42, 59; **The Driving Test**, page 25.

4 Move away: **Learn to Drive**, pages 38, 39, 50, 51, 52, 53, 89, 90; **The Driving Test**, page 27.

5 Emergency stop: **Learn to Drive**, pages 57, 58; **The Driving Test**, page 33.

6 Reverse to left or right: **Learn to Drive**, pages 95, 96, 97, 98; **The Driving Test**, page 34.

7 Turn in the road: **Learn to Drive**, pages 94, 95; **The Driving Test**, page 37.

8 Reverse Parking: **Learn to Drive**, pages 99, 100; **The Driving Test**, page 35.

9 Use of mirrors: **Learn to Drive**, pages 37, 38, 66, 67, 68, 107, 108, 109, 129, 130, 159, 163; **The Driving Test**, page 28.

10 Give appropriate signals: **Learn to Drive**, pages 37, 59, 66, 68, 107, 108, 109, 110; **The Driving Test**, page 29.

11 Response to signs and signals: **Learn to Drive**, pages 106, 115, 119, 120, 121, 122, 123, 130; **The Driving Test**, page 30.

12 Use of speed: **Learn to Drive**, pages 106, 149, 150, 155, 156, 157, 165, 166, 169, 173, 174; **The Driving Test**, page 31

13 Following distance: **Learn to Drive**, page 105; **The Driving Test**, page 44.

14 Maintaining progress: **Learn to Drive**, pages 128, 131, 207, 208, **The Driving Test**, page 32.

15 Junctions:
approach speed: **Learn to Drive**, pages 66, 67, 68, 72, 78, 81; **The Driving Test**, pages 39, 40.
observation: **Learn to Drive**, pages 78, 80, 81, 131, 132, 133; **The Driving Test**, page 39.

Sample appointment/process card

APPOINTMENTS

Day	Date	Time	£	Sig.

48 Hours Notice of Cancellation is Required.

Name: ....

Address: ....

....

Driver Number: ....

General Information

Before your first lesson make sure you can read a number plate from 67 feet (20.5m).

Read lessons 1 & 2 of 'Learn to Drive', completing the Checkpoints.

Please bring your driving licence with you on your lessons.

COURSE OUTLINE

Stage 1 Before You Drive

Eyesight Checked: .... [ ]

Licence Checked: .... [ ]

Stage 2 Get to Know The Car

Cockpit Drill [ ]

Precautions/Starting Engine [ ]

Stage 3 Starting to Drive

Moving off [ ]

Changing up and down the gears [ ]

Speed and Steering [ ]

Basic M S M Routines [ ]

Stopping and Parking [ ]

Stage 4 Methodical Practice

Ex. 1 Moving Off [ ]

Ex. 2 Moving Off Downhill [ ]

Ex. 3 Changing Up the Gears [ ]

Ex. 4 Changing Down the Gears [ ]

Ex. 5 Braking/Pausing/Stopping [ ]

Ex. 6 Emergency Stop [ ]

Ex. 7 Steering [ ]

Stage 5 Gaining Confidence

M S M and P S L Routines [ ]

Position Turning Left/Right Corners [ ]

Approaching and Emerging Junctions [ ]

Giving Way/Holdback Positions [ ]

Stage 6 Reversing and Manoeuvering

Ex. 1 Low Speed Clutch Control [ ]

Ex. 2 Moving from Behind Parked Car [ ]

Ex. 3 Reversing in a Straight Line [ ]

Ex. 4 Driving into a Parking Space [ ]

Ex. 5 Turning the Car round [ ]

Ex. 6 Reversing to the Left [ ]

Ex. 7 Reversing to the Right [ ]

Ex. 8 Reverse Parking [ ]

Stage 7 Commonsense and Experience

Following Others Safely [ ]

Acting Promptly on Signals [ ]

Making Effective use of Mirrors [ ]

Making proper use of Signals [ ]

Dealing with Pedestrian Crossings [ ]

Dealing with Traffic Lights [ ]

Driving in Lanes [ ]

Dealing with Roundabout [ ]

Overtaking Safely [ ]

Dealing with Level Crossings [ ]

Stage 8 Learning to Anticipate

Using Speed Correctly [ ]

Anticipating the action of others [ ]

Being Patient and Considerate [ ]

Avoiding Accidents [ ]

Concentrate when Driving [ ]

Using Eye Contact [ ]

Anticipating Large Vehicles [ ]

Pedestrians/Cyclists/Animals [ ]

Poor Visibility/Weather Conditions [ ]

Vehicle Instability [ ]

Stage 9 Higher Speeds/Simple Mechanics

Route Planning [ ]

Driving at Higher Speeds [ ]

Reducing the Risk of Breakdown [ ]

How to Change a Wheel [ ]

What to do if You Break Down [ ]

Stage 10 The Driving Test

Applying for the Test [ ]

Taking the Test [ ]

After the Test [ ]

✳ ✳ ✳

Theory Test Passed on: .... [ ]

Practical Test at: .... [ ]

Date: .... Time: .... am/pm

When you go for your driving test, please remember to bring your driving licence.

Theory Test pass certificate and I.D. [ ]

Copyright Autodriva 1998

LEARN TO **DRIVE** IN 10 EASY STAGES

WITH

We Follow The
DSA
Code of Practice

Copyright Autodriva 1998

22	Use of ancillary controls
21	Anticipation others
20	Safe psn: normal stops
19	Action: pcd crossing
18	Allow adequate clearances
17	Psn: lane discipline
17	Psn: normal driving
16	Other vehicles: crossing path
16	Other vehicles: meeting
16	Other vehicles: overtaking
15	Jnct: right corner cut
15	Jnct: psn before right
15	Jnct: psn before left
15	Jnct: observation
15	Jncts: speed on approach
14	Avoid hesitancy
14	Make progress
13	Safe distance behind others
12	Exercise care/use of speed
11	Action: signs/markings/others
10	Give signals correctly
9	Effective use of mirrors
8	Reverse park
7	Turn in the road
6	Reverse to right or left
5	Emergency stop
4	Move away safely u/control
3	Use of steering
3	Use of handbrake
3	Use of footbrake
3	Use of gears
3	Use of clutch
3	Use of accelerator
2	Precautions starting engine
1	Meet eyesight requirements

Your instructor will record any areas for revision. To locate the correct procedures match the code number with the revision chart in '**Learn to Drive in 10 Easy Stages**'

INSTRUCTOR MARKING CODE

T = Teaching : F = Fair : G = Good
/ = Minor Error : X = Serious Faults

APPOINTMENTS

Day	Date	Time	£	Sig.

Index